What Next?

What Next?

Ideas for Worship, Thought, Discussion, Action

PETER COTTERELL

Marshall, Morgan & Scott

LAKELAND
Marshall, Morgan & Scott
a member of the Pentos group
1 Bath Street, London EC1V 9LB

ISBN 0 551 00798 2

Printed in Great Britain by Cox & Wyman Ltd,
London, Reading and Fakenham

For Geraldine, Anne and Janet
The family God has given me

Contents

An Explanation

This book is for young people. Of course you can be young at fifty and old at nineteen but young people are always people who are prepared to grow. So this is a book for Christians who want to grow. It has been written because I want to grow, too.

The eleven chapters deal with prayer and pain, the church and success, freewill and marriage. Each chapter could be used as the basis for maybe a month of discussions. There are skits, one-act plays, scattered through the book. If you use them don't spoil them by making them over-elaborate. Some of them can be ad-libbed. Some can be read. All of them have been used in church.

Most of the Bible passages given are from Dr Kenneth Taylor's paraphrased *Living Bible*. Unrepentantly I consider this a magnificent piece of work. It *is* a paraphrase. It has the inestimable advantage for me that I understand it. My thanks to Dr Taylor for permission to use it here.

P.C.

The Way to Up is Down

I was dreaming I suppose and yet me dream was very odd
'cos I thought I saw the angels standing round the throne of
  God.
Each one wore a crown of gold and sang like fifty choirs in
  one
and I felt I'd like to join them when me life on earth was
  done.

Course, I couldn't be an angel, but perhaps I'd find a place
where I'd always hear the angels and just sometimes see
  God's face.
If I sat beside the choir I'd be no trouble on me own
and it really would be heaven to see God upon 'is throne.

It was just a simple question that I asked the angel host,
'Which way *is* the way to heaven, that's what worries me the
  most?'
You'd expect a simple answer from an angel with a crown,
But he said 'There's only one way, and the way to up is
  down.'

Well, I didn't understand it, so I asked 'im once again,
'Be an angel, mate, and tell me which way's best for sinful
  men?'
But the angel choir turned round as one, and with one joyful
  shout
they replied: 'The way to up is down and the way to in is
  out.'

I tried again, I thought maybe they didn't understand:
' 'ere mates what *is* the way to God and to the Promised
  Land?'

Then the angel boss stood out and whispered to me, soft as
    breath:
'The way to up is down, lad, and the way to life is death.

If you save your life you'll lose it' I could hear the angel say,
'If you think you see, you're blind, but if you ask to see, you
    may.
He who thinks he's fit for heav'n is on the downward path to
    hell,
for the poor man shall be rich and soon the sick man shall be
    well.'

Then the angels gathered round and sang the song I can't
    forget;
though I haven't understood it, I shall understand it yet:
'God's ways aren't the same as your ways and his thoughts
    are different too,
for the way to up was down for Christ, and the way is down
    for you.'

CHAPTER 1

What's Wrong?

Some years back, *The Times* of London featured a lengthy correspondence on the subject, 'What's wrong with the world?' There were all kinds of suggestions, but the final letter, from G. K. Chesterton, answered the question in just two words:

> Dear Sir,
>   What's wrong with the world?
>   I am.
>   Yours faithfully,
>   G. K. Chesterton

Now there can be no doubt at all that technically speaking we do live in an amazing world. Televison, pocket calculators, communication satellites, nuclear power, supersonic aircraft and even a man on the moon just as predicted. And yet, when we compare the fabulous efficiency of these scientific achievements with our total failure in trying to get Boris to live with Horace, all the euphoria evaporates. Horace just won't live with Boris and nothing we do seems to have the power to change his mind. The difference between getting Boris to change his mind and getting him to the moon is obvious enough. Getting him to the moon is simply a matter of technology, of payloads and power ratios. Getting Boris to live with Horace is a matter of temperament. Machinery is amenable, people are temperamental: ninety per cent temper and ten per cent mental.

In fact, just so soon as the human factor is fed into the computer, all the fuses blow. There's no programme to deal with human behaviour. It can't be quantified, it defies prediction. Just so soon as I feel that I understand how my friends work, what makes them tick, some new aberration appears and I have to start my analysis all over again. I remember the story that used to be attributed to Professors Haldane and Huxley. They were dining together in a London hotel, arguing as usual about some point of philosophy, when Huxley said, rather irritably,

'It's no use going on with this argument; I know just what you're going to say next and just what you're going to do next.'

Haldane stood up without a word, walked to the middle of the dining-room and solemnly stood on his head. Then he walked back to their table and retorted,

'That's just to show you that you don't know what I'm going to do next!'

Man *is* unpredictable. He *is* illogical. He will go on strike, knowing that his action will likely wreck the company that pays his salary that buys his daily bread. He will dive into a river to rescue a struggling child even though he can't swim. He will climb a mountain just because. He will share his inadequate mouthful with his fellow prisoner while his captor plans the extermination of both. What a mixture he is! But he is more than a mixture: he is all mixed up. And he knows it. He can't put his finger on just what is wrong, but he knows. And he spends his life looking for the solution: the one 'thing' that will make life happy.

That's the word: happy. Man isn't happy. It's not hedonism, the pursuit of happiness that bothers him, simply that he isn't happy. And there doesn't seem to be any formula for becoming happy. The scientists are no happier than he is. Not even the rich seem happier than he is. Their problems are very different, but they've got them all right. Wouldn't have his job for a fortune!

What *is* man, that he can be so mixed up?

WHAT THE BIBLE SAYS ABOUT IT

Psalm 8
O Lord our God, the majesty and glory of your name
    fills all the earth and overflows the heavens.

You have taught the little children to praise you perfectly.
May their example shame and silence your enemies!

When I look up into the night skies
      and see the work of your fingers—
      the moon and the stars you have made—
      I cannot understand how you can bother with puny
         man,
      to pay attention to him!
And yet you have made him only a little lower than the
         angels,
      and placed a crown of glory and honour upon his
         head.

You have put him in charge of everything you made;
      everything is put under his authority;
      all sheep and oxen, and wild animals too,
      the birds and fish, and all the life in the sea.

O Jehovah, our Lord,
the majesty and glory of your name fills the earth.

Job 25.2–6
God is powerful and dreadful. He enforces peace in heaven.
Who is able to number his hosts of angels? And his light
shines down on all the earth. How can mere man stand
before God and claim to be righteous? Who in all the earth
can boast that he is clean?

MORE LIGHT ON THE PROBLEM

So here is man: on the one hand we can never tell what he
might try to do next, he is irresponsible, unpredictable, at
one moment evil, depraved, repellent, and suddenly there
flashes from him pure love, beauty of thought or action. We
pause to curse man's inhumanity and even as we pause he
does something unexpectedly glorious that turns curse into
blessing. Mixed up!

And because man is mixed up, so is the world in which

God has put him. People in London and New York go about their business unconcerned that as they do so children are starving to death in what they are pleased to call the Third World ... at any rate it certainly isn't *their* world. While Western man tackles his T-bone steak or his bacon-and-eggs he worries about his indigestion and his income tax with no real concern for the world where stomach pains come from starvation and there is no income to be taxed. And then, when the poor, confused, exploited world begins to hit out at him, when his resources begin to dry up, he thinks grandiloquently of transferring the scene of his operations to another planet which might appreciate his genius more ... and where there will be no Third World or income tax ...

SOUND OF ROCKET ENGINES for 10 seconds; FADE TO BACK-GROUND

GEORGE: That's queer ... the clock's stopped ... wonder what caused that? Hello! The other clock's stopped, too ... everything else seems to be normal though. Must be a circuit break ... if it is, we'll have Mission Control on to us in a minute ... but I wonder why the fault doesn't show on the computer?

GOD: It's not a circuit break. It won't show up on your computer. And you *won't* have Mission Control on to you in a minute. I've suspended time.

GEORGE: You've suspended time? And who on earth might you be?

GOD: I'm not on earth, and it's of no concern to you who I am. You don't believe in me.

GEORGE: (*involuntarily*) Oh God!

GOD: (*drily*) Quite!

GEORGE: Look, whoever you are you can't suspend time. (*a little superior now*) Of course I appreciate that time is not an absolute ... I do have my Master's degree in science and (*definitely pompous*) I'm working towards my PH.D.

GOD: I know ... theism, pantheism and now Ph.Deism.

14

When will you take time to learn how little you have learned? Now then, go back! Go back to earth!

GEORGE: Go back? You don't seem to understand ... we're on the first ever trip to land permanent settlers on Mars. (*enthusiastic*) Every problem has been solved and now the greatest event in the history of the world is about to take place.

GOD: The greatest event in the history of the world took place two thousand years ago ... Go back!

GEORGE: But I can't go back. There is no provision in our programme for going back. I don't even know *how* to go back.

GOD: So there is something you don't know?

GEORGE: Well ... there are small pockets of knowledge still denied to us, but they are rapidly yielding to the determined onslaught of our intellectuals; most disease is already under control ...

GOD: (*interrupts*) ... but not the common cold, I understand ...

GEORGE: (*hurries on*) ... and we have conquered the problem of living in the potentially hostile environment of Mars ...

GOD: (*interrupts again*) ... although you don't seem to be able to live in the environment of your wife ...

GEORGE: (*caught off guard*) How do you know about my ... Anyway, as I said, we can't go back. We go to Mars to establish the first extra-terrestrial outpost of scientific learning.

GOD: You go to Mars to establish yet one more outpost of savage ignorance. (*firmly*) No, I'm sorry, we've decided that you have gone far enough. You have polluted your own world and now you plan on polluting my world. Go back!

GEORGE: (*frightened*) This is impossible ... how does he get through to me? Everything seems normal ... just the clocks stopped (*pause, then a gasp*) ... and my heart ... there's no beat ... no pulse ... nothing. (*addresses God*) Who *are* you?

GOD: You do not know my Name, and I will not tell it to you. You don't believe in me. Now, go back.

15

In your cabin there you'll find a Book. One of your predecessors read from it when he came this way a few years back. Read it ... you may learn something. Something that's *really* important.

Go back ... and don't try to make this trip again. It won't be permitted.

SOUND OF ROCKET ENGINES PICKS UP AGAIN

GEORGE: Hey ... the clocks have started again ... and my pulse has come back ... and the engines ... Everything's back to normal. I must have passed out for a moment ... What's that book doing there ... Psalms ... Psalm 131 ...

> 'Lord, I am not proud and haughty.
> I don't think myself better than others.
> I don't pretend to "know it all".
> I am quiet now before the Lord ...'

It must have been ... God?
And he's right ... we've turned round ...
We're headed back to Earth ... we *are* going back!

FADE OUT SOUND OF ENGINE

*   *   *

We certainly have made a mess of *this* world. And we could well understand that God wouldn't want us to carry our chaos out into the universe around us. We don't know how many other worlds there are out there, if any of them have life like the life we know, if that life has fallen, as ours has. Fallen. It's a good word for describing the world we now have to try to live in. A world with weeds and war, cancer and chaos, kings, presidents, prime ministers, governments, parliaments and councils and no one capable of ruling. Because the world has fallen ...

*   *   *

But I don't want to.
What has that got to do with me? You have to.
But I have a will of my own. I don't want to, I tell you.
Whether you want to or not, you'll still do it.
Yes ... I know that. You're right. But ... who are you? You who are always close to me. Who am I arguing with?

16

You're arguing with yourself. I am you. You are me.
Then can't I *make* you set me free? If you are *really* me how
   can we disagree? It doesn't make sense.
I never could make sense; I don't even try.
Ah! Now I know you. You are sin, which lives in me.
*I am sin which lives in you. I am your past. And your past is
   full of me.*
And it is because of you that I cannot do what I want to do.
   But now I know who you are I can be free of you.
   It's not I who do all these wrong things. It's you.
But I am stronger than you are.
I know that. But there is one who is stronger.
Oh yes; my master. Evil lies close at hand.
I know him, too. But there is a yet stronger.
Indeed? Who *will deliver you?*
Who will deliver me?
I thank God, Jesus Christ . . .   (Romans 7.13–25).

*   *   *

Who is going to deliver me? That's the question that most of
us ask at some time or other. When the going gets tough.
Before our consciences get hardened or our hopes disappointed once too often. Who will deliver us? We soon discover that we can't deliver ourselves. Politics? I lived in an
African country for almost twenty years under a regime that
has been fairly called oppressive. The inevitable revolution
came. The Head of State was imprisoned, then murdered. So
was the next Head of State . . . and the next. The new regime,
set up to put right the wrongs of established feudalism,
began by abolishing Parliament and soon banished justice
altogether, so that their last end was worse than their first.
No, we won't find freedom in politics.

    The church then?

*   *   *

Opening Time
We stood outside the chapel but we wanted to get in,
Just Bill and me, we'd come to try to get rid of our sin;
We rang the bell and shouted, but no one seemed to hear,

It was early Monday evening, so we went and 'ad a beer.
Well, the public house was open, and they welcomed Bill an'
me,
But they close the church on Monday, while the Vicar 'as 'is
tea.

We tried again on Tuesday and we rang the bell at nine.
You'd 'ave thought that they'd be open, all the shops was
doin' fine.
Still, we waited for an hour 'till at last the Vicar come,
Wiv 'is collar put on backwards and a dress on like me
mum;
He said 'Come again on Wednesday, I have things that I
must do.'
So we walked off quite respectful and we visited the zoo,
'cos the zoo is open Tuesdays and they're glad to have you
in,
(though they don't know how to help you if you want to lose
your sin).
We sat and watched the monkeys, one was searching for a
bug,
But they close the church on Tuesday while the Vicar knits a
rug.

We tried again on Wednesday, but the Vicar wasn't there . . .
No, I'm wrong, 'e come at half-past-eight and said a little
prayer;
'E didn't notice Bill an' me, 'e was in an' out so quick,
So we went to see the doctor, Bill was feeling kind of sick . . .
Well, the doctor didn't tell us to come back another day.
I suppose 'e'd get in trouble if 'e sent the sick away.

So, on Thursday and on Friday and on Saturday we came,
And the answer to our question every day was just the same,
'Come tomorrow, I'm too busy, I'm a-reading of a book,
Come tomorrow with your sins and maybe then I'll have a
look.'
Well, tomorrow will be Sunday and the Vicar will be there,
But 'e won't find Bill an' me in church a-kneelin' down for
prayer;

Maybe heaven *is* for sinners, men like Bill an' men like me,
But they close the church on Monday while the Vicar 'as 'is tea.

* * *

What can God do for the Bills of this world? Make things a bit easier for him in a practical sort of way? Some of us think, subconsciously, of God as a kind of super-Socialist whose goal is the redistribution of the world's wealth so that we all get what we would estimate to be our fair share.

A friend of mine was in the Northern Frontier District of Kenya, talking with a group of Galla people. They sat in a neighbourly sort of way around a flickering fire. One of them asked him:

'Where do you come from?'

'I come from the village of London.'

'In the village of London, how many hours each day do the women spend going down to the river to fetch water?'

The men all knew that this was the major work of *their* women folk, most of whom travelled an average of four hours each day, fetching water from the muddy stream that was their only water supply. My friend thought a moment – how could he explain a tap? Then:

'In the houses of the village of London, there is a hole in the wall. When the women want water, it comes for them through the hole.'

The men thought about this for a few moments, and then one objected:

'But this, surely, is for the rich people of the village of London. How many hours each day do the poor women spend in fetching water?'

'No, even for the poor people of the village of London, there is a hole in the wall of each house, and water comes out of the hole when it is wanted.'

Silence. Then, from out of the darkness one of the men whispered:

'How happy must be the people of the village of London!'

How could my friend explain that in the village of London, with miracles so extraordinary that no words could describe them, no eloquence make these people even believe in their existence, people were not merely not happy, but even desperately miserable. And more: how could he convince them that even if this same miracle could be provided for them ... a miraculous hole-in-the-wall in every hut ... *they* would not be content either.

God does something more profound than re-distributing wealth. (Don't get the idea that he approves of our one-sided economic situation, either. But he knows that re-distribution is only a temporary measure: soon mixed-up-fallen-man will put the distribution back the way *he* wants it.) God doesn't change the outside: he changes man inside.

What's wrong with the world? I am. God puts the 'I' right.

THINK IT OVER

1. Back in the Old Testament, the Jewish people were waiting to receive the Ten Commandments and the rest of the Law. Before they received the commandments and again after receiving them they promised: 'We'll do everything that God says' (Exodus 19.8 and 24.7).

But they didn't (Exodus 32.1–6).

Look at Romans 7.9: how is it possible for a law actually to encourage sin? Think what happens when children are told, 'Don't touch the books!' What does the idea of the Fall have to say in explanation of this behaviour in children?

2. Which of the following do most people seem to want? Try listing them in order of people's preference.

Money	Happiness
Fame	Health
Complete security	Friends

Talk about this list. Is there a difference in the preferences shown by men and women? By young people and older people? Do values seem to change? If so, why?

CHAPTER 2

Chosen to be Free

Surely there's something wrong with that title: how can I be *chosen* to be free? If someone else does the choosing then surely I'm not free?

But it's God doing the choosing. God chooses me, so that I can be free. How can he be God if he isn't free to choose? How can he be God if he has to wait for my decisions before he can take his decisions?

Some people solve the problem by stating flatly that we don't have free will, we can't really choose, freedom is an illusion. Oddly enough the most thorough-going material-istic atheists say that and so do a lot of thorough-going Christians. But it won't do. I think it was Dr Johnson (and this book won't have a lot of learned footnotes so I don't intend taking time to look up all these interesting remi-niscences of mine), I think it was Dr Johnson who settled the matter for me quite simply: he said:

'Sir, we know we have free will.'

So we do, and so we have. But.

But not entirely free. I'll grant you that. We're not as free as some of us think we are, and we're not as chained up as some of us think we are. Some things we *can* decide to do, while there are many choices that we're just not free to make. I can choose whether I'll buy a blue Hillman or a green Ford, although I probably am not free to choose a Rolls-Royce. I am free to repent. In Acts 2, which details the events of the Pentecostal outpouring of the Holy Spirit, we hear Peter commanding his listeners: 'Repent!' He wasn't play-acting. He was telling them to do something that they ought to do.

But ... that word again ... but hadn't God already de-cided who should be able to repent? And weren't they the ones who *did* repent? So how were they free? There's the snag, once again. Because God did have a plan; Peter speaks about that, too:

'. . . this Jesus, delivered up according to the definite plan and foreknowledge of God, you crucified and killed . . .' (Acts 2.23).

So if God had a plan, and he had foreknowledge, knowledge *before*, the people involved in crucifying Jesus had no free choice. Although they would have said with Dr Johnson,

'Sir, we *know* we have free will.'

It's all rather confusing.

WHAT THE BIBLE SAYS ABOUT IT

Romans 8.26–31
The Holy Spirit helps us with our daily problems and in our praying. For we don't even know what we should pray for, nor how to pray as we should; but the Holy Spirit prays for us with such feeling that it cannot be expressed in words. And the Father who knows all hearts knows, of course, what the Spirit is saying as he pleads for us in harmony with God's own will. And we know that all that happens to us is working for our good if we love God and are fitting into his plans.

For from the very beginning God decided that those who came to him – and all along he knew who would – should become like his Son, so that his Son would be the First, with many brothers. And having chosen us, he called us to come to him; and when we came, he declared us 'not guilty', filled us with Christ's goodness, gave us right standing with himself, and promised us his glory.

What can we ever say to such wonderful things as these?

Romans 9.10–14
God told Rebecca that Esau, the child born first, would be a servant to Jacob, his twin brother . . . and God said this before the children were even born, before they had done anything either good or bad. This proves that God was

doing what he had decided from the beginning; it was not because of what the children did but because of what God wanted and chose. Was God being unfair? Of course not.

THINKING IT THROUGH

Or maybe God *was* being unfair? If God knows who will come to him before they are even called, and if Jacob was given all the privileges before he was born, wasn't that hard ... not on the ones who were chosen, and not on Jacob, but on those who weren't chosen, and on Esau? There's the whole problem located for us in one word: *before.* Can we deal with the problem of the before? I'm not sure that we can, but occasionally we get glimpses of the truth: we sense that we're almost at the answer, but the answer is a bit like the new elements that have been produced in our nuclear research programmes: they disappear as soon as you look at them.

Here's C. S. Lewis on the subject:

You must remember that man takes time as an ultimate reality. He supposes that the Enemy (Screwtape's enemy, God), like himself, sees some things as present, remembers others as past, and anticipates others as future; or even if he believes that the Enemy does not see things that way, yet, in his heart of hearts, he regards this as a peculiarity of the Enemy's mode of perception – he doesn't really think that things as the Enemy sees them are things as they are!

He would add that the weather on a given day can be traced back through its causes to the original creation of matter itself – so that the whole thing, both on the human and on the material side, is given 'from the word go'. What he ought to say, of course, is that the problem of adapting the particular weather to the particular prayers is merely the appearance, at two points in his temporal mode of perception, of the total problem of adapting the whole spiritual universe to the whole corporeal universe;

that their kind of consciousness forces them to encounter the whole, self-consistent creative act as a series of successive events. *Why* that creative act leaves room for their free will is the problem of problems, the secret behind the Enemy's nonsense about 'Love'. *How* it does so is no problem at all; for the Enemy does not *foresee* the humans making their free contributions in a future, but *sees* them doing so in His unbounded Now. And obviously to watch a man doing something is not to make him do it.

This is helpful as a hint: it doesn't answer all the questions, but it does begin to deal with the problem of *before*. Let's try again: a memory that has stayed with me for twenty-five years must have something to commend it. It was Tom Rees, trying to answer this same question about our freedom. I'm quoting from memory, but I think I'm about right:

I was out in the car with my wife, Jean, and we were listening to the radio; it was one of those quiz games – Twenty Questions. It was about the third question, and as soon as they started, I said to Jean:
  'They're not going to get it.'
  'How do you know?' she said. 'They might get it.'
  'They're *not* going to get it,' I said. And we listened while their questions added up.
  'It's no use, they won't get it: they *can't* get it.'
  'Tom, don't be ridiculous; how can you possibly know?'
  'They won't get it!'
  And they didn't get it. Rather smugly I told Jean: 'See, I knew they weren't going to get it. They couldn't possibly have got it.'
  Jean was quite upset by now: 'Tom, you just guessed, you couldn't possibly *know*.'
  '*I knew*. They couldn't possibly guess it. You see, this is a recorded programme: I heard it last night!'

Another glimpse. Again pointing to this question of time. We see time as flowing in one direction: yesterday, today, tomorrow, Monday, Tuesday, Wednesday. And we accept the convenient fiction that there are always sixty seconds in a minute and sixty minutes in an hour. Anyone who hates the dentist's chair as much as I do will know that some hours have at least one hundred and twenty minutes in them, but annoyingly holiday weeks seem only to have five days.

Even so, we are only getting glimpses of the facts here. Actually it is a bit of a help being a physicist: in physics we are quite used to the idea that one minute doesn't always have sixty seconds to it: if you are in a space ship travelling fast enough, or better still can hitch a ride on an electron, you will find that your seconds stretch out astonishingly . . . at least, when compared with other people's seconds.

So a second doesn't always last for a second . . . a second on *our* time scale, that is.

But another pointer from physics: we never see things *as they are*, we only see them *as they were*. And we can only hear what George *said*, never what he *is saying*. Now, light travels rather quickly: 186,000 miles in every second. Sound is quite a tortoise by comparison: one fifth of a mile per second or just over 700 miles per hour. So if George was to stand on the sun (I know he couldn't, but *if*) and then shouted (there'd be plenty to make him shout) then you would *see* him from the earth (if you had a good enough telescope), with his mouth open, about eight minutes later, and you would *hear* the shout (if you had a good enough ear and if sound could travel through space, which it can't, but *if*) some thirty-six hours later. And you might say:

'I can see George shouting.'

and you might add, after a couple of days,

'I can hear George shouting.'

but George *isn't* shouting: he *shouted*.

Of course, if we put George away out on one of the stars we could see George long after he was dead and buried. Or if we could join George on his star then we could watch the Battle of Waterloo or see Moses climbing Mount Sinai or join Gautama the Buddha under his Bo tree simply by changing our star. We would see it in *our* NOW, although it would be the *Earth*'s THEN.

So it really isn't too difficult to imagine ourselves seeing the past in the present. *God* can go one stage further: he sees both past and future in his own NOW.

So we get another glimpse of a different kind of world, where some of the logical problems that perplex us don't exist. Just because there is no yesterday and no tomorrow.

But most of us probably still feel that any theory we hold about free-will against God's sovereignty *ought* to be logical. And it doesn't seem logical to allow God to do all the choosing when I'm supposed to be free to choose for myself. The time thing helps, but shouldn't a good theory be logical? Well, physics again (if you find this physics thing unhelpful skip the next paragraph).

Physics talks a great deal about electrons: tiny 'particles' which we often think of as if they were bullets loaded with electricity. Some parts of physics talk about these electrons as if they were spheres whirling round the atoms of which matter is made. It's convenient sometimes to think of electrons in that way. It's convenient to think of light like that, too. Photons of light, also like bullets, hurtling around in straight lines, casting nice sharp shadows when an obstruction gets in the way. But light doesn't always behave like photon bullets. And electrons don't always behave like tiny spheres. Sometimes the bullets and spheres seem to disappear and instead we find ourselves talking about light 'waves'. Now a bullet isn't a wave. It could be part of a wave, but it isn't a wave. A bullet is *here* and not *there*: it hits the bullseye in the target or it scores an outer, but it can't do both. A wave isn't just *here* or *there*: it's everywhere. So, is an electron a particle or a wave? Is a photon a particle or a wave? And the physicist cheerfully answers, 'It's both.'

But it isn't logical! Surely it must be either the one or the other? And the physicist answers:

'I know it isn't logical: but it works. To explain the facts about the electron we have to talk about the *mass* of the particle and its *wavelength*. Maybe one day we'll get closer to understanding what's really going on in the atom and then we'll be able to clear up the logic. But for the present, with the knowledge we now have, this is the best we can do.'

And that's how it is with God and freedom and his sovereignty. *He* has to be in control. *I* have to be free. Maybe one day we'll understand how both can be true at once. Till then we'll have to put up with a few glimpses into the answer: time that can vary, a present with no past and no future, the truths of the Bible only properly presented when we accept a paradox.

CHOSEN TO BE FREE

James and Oliver are both preachers, one Presbyterian and the other Baptist. At least, James is as strongly Predestinarian as Oliver is a Free-willer. Each of them clutches a large Bible. They walk in from opposite sides and meet in the centre:

JAMES/OLIVER: (*together*) Hello there, brother! You must be a preacher!

JAMES: Yes indeed . . . just moved in last month.

OLIVER: Me too!

JAMES: There's a destiny in these things . . .

OLIVER: There certainly is . . . We must meet again . . . (*they walk off in opposite directions, circle around and meet once again in the centre*)

JAMES: Hello again . . . er . . . which church did you say you were from?

OLIVER: I didn't say. You didn't ask.

JAMES: Well, which church *are* you from?

OLIVER: The Reformed Separated John Knox Presbyterian. What about you?

JAMES: Beulah Street Independent Full-Bible Baptist.

OLIVER: Oh . . . We must meet again . . . (*they walk off as before, circle round and meet in the centre*)

JAMES: Did you say that you are at the Reformed Separated John Knox Presbyterian church?

OLIVER: I did. I am.

JAMES: Not the Full-Gospel Anti-Penultimate Wesleyan church?

OLIVER: Nope!

JAMES: Oh . . . We must meet again. (*they walk off as before, circle, and meet in the centre*)

JAMES: I've been thinking about what you said . . . about being at the Reformed Separated John Knox Presbyterian church. You mean that you believe in . . . predestination? And election?

OLIVER: Yup!

JAMES: You mean, you don't believe in free-will?

OLIVER: Of course not . . . I'm married.

JAMES: Oh . . . Well, we must meet again. (*they walk off as before, circle and meet in the centre*). Say, it's ecumenical Sunday next Sunday. How would you feel about exchanging pulpits? You preach in my church and I'll preach in yours. How about that?

OLIVER: Okay. We must meet again . . . (*they walk off, circle around a bit. Each picks up a folder of sermon notes, prominently labelled. Oliver's is labelled* 'The perfection of election and the elation of predestination' *and James' folder is labelled* 'Free-will proved: fifty pithy points for progressive preachers'.

They meet again in the centre; they are on their way to preach in one another's churches.)

JAMES: Hello there! What a marvellous morning!

OLIVER: It is indeed . . .

JAMES: A wonderful day! And how does it feel to be visiting the Beulah Street Independent Full-Bible Baptist church?

OLIVER: (*suddenly and uncharacteristically verbose*) Do you realise, my dear friend, that it has been ordained from all eternity, that on this day, on this sabbath day, *you* should preach in *my* church, and *I* should preach in *yours*?!

JAMES: (*taken aback; he hadn't thought of it like that at all!*) Oh . . . is that so . . .? (*pause . . . thinks*) Well . . . I won't do it.

OLIVER: You won't do it?

JAMES: (*decided*) No . . . I won't do it. I'll preach in my own church. (*turns around and goes back the way he came and exits.*)

OLIVER: (*definitely perplexed, scratches his head*) It must have been ordained from all eternity that we *shouldn't* preach in each other's churches ... (*walks off sadly in the direction he had come from, and exits*)

THINK IT OVER

1. In Exodus 3.13–15 we have a powerful insight into the nature of God, given to us through the revelation of His Name, 'I AM'. The Name (which is never pronounced by the Jew) comes from a Hebrew word which means 'to exist'. The Name can be translated in many different ways: 'I am what I am', 'I am what I will be', 'I will be what I will be', and so on. The point is simply that God IS. He doesn't change as we do.

Jesus takes up the same idea in John 8.58: 'Before Abraham *was,* I *am.*' Why does this strange name, 'I am', encourage us when things seem to be going wrong? What was God trying to teach Moses and the Jews when he revealed this name to them? Look at Jesus' use of the same Name in John's gospel (look up the seven 'I ams' of the gospel, and his other uses of this phrase).

2. I don't know what may happen to me tomorrow. God does. Why doesn't he tell me?

3. How detailed is God's 'definite plan' mentioned in Acts 2.23?

4. Once when Donald Barnhouse was on his travels, visiting missionaries all over the world, he came to some missionaries working in a very tough area. He shared with them some of the great stories of God's work in other parts of the world. But when he finished talking, one of the missionaries simply burst into tears:

'We're no use here. Everywhere else God is at work, but there must be something wrong with us. We have been here for eleven years and there's not even one convert.'

Donald Barnhouse (a Presbyterian!) asked her:

'Now listen, when Christ finally takes his church to glory, who will he take?'

'All those who are his.'

'How many of his will be missing?'

'None.'

'Then if God has seen fit to send you to a place where you see no results from your labours why do you worry about the lack of results, the absence of converts? Your task is to preach the Good News.'

The girl was encouraged by what he said. But what is the danger of that way of thinking?

5. William Carey was told in 1792:

'If God means to convert the heathen he can do it without you.' So he can. Why *should* we tell others about Christ?

what would you think if you heard an ear say, 'I am not part of the body because I am only an ear and not an eye?' Would that make it any less a part of the body? Suppose the whole body were an eye – then how would you hear? Or if your whole body were just one big ear, how would you smell anything?

But that isn't the way God has made us. He has made many parts for our bodies and has put each part just where he wants it. What a strange thing a body would be if it had only one part! So he has made many parts, but still there is only one body.

The eye can never say to the hand, 'I don't need you.' The head can't say to the feet, 'I don't need you.'

And some of the parts that seem weakest and least important are really the most necessary. Yes, we are especially glad to have some parts that seem rather odd! . . .

Now here is what I am trying to say: All of you together are the one body of Christ and each one of you is a separate and necessary part of it.

THINKING IT THROUGH

Semantics. That's simply the study of *meaning*. The meaning of a word is more than what the dictionary says. Take the word 'brother'. According to the dictionary he is: 'a male, related to others (male or female) as the child of the same parents or parent.'

That's all right as far as it goes. But it doesn't tell me much about Cliff, my twin brother. Cliff, who ran away from home with me (six years old, and running away from home!), and broke his leg twice, and knelt with me as we gave ourselves to God and . . . well, *that's* Cliff. Not the dictionary meaning. The meaning of a word is really decided for us by its associations. The word 'brother', for me, means Cliff. The word 'table' means a good meal to the man with an appetite, or a multiplication table to the children going to school, or maybe even a water table to a geologist.

The word 'church'. It often means wooden pews, tedious

services, Gothic architecture and a strange language of thees and thous, memories of church services attended in the past. But the first Christian churches weren't like that at all. Christians first met in the homes of the better-off members of the church. Because *their* homes would be bigger, of course. There was a church in Philemon's home and another in the home of Aquila and Priscilla. So the idea of the house church isn't new at all.

Of course, the word 'church', as used in the New Testament, never means a bricks-and-mortar building. It means the Christians who met together to worship God. The Greek word *ekklēsia* (from which we get our clumsy word 'ecclesiastical') is made up of two parts, meaning 'called out'. The church is made up of people, ordinary people, called out of an ungodly way of life to live the life of eternity.

We sometimes divide the world-wide, centuries-old church into the 'church militant' and the 'church triumphant'. The church militant is made up of all Christians still living in this world. The church triumphant consists of all Christians who have 'died', that is, have passed beyond our experience of alternating victory and defeat and into the marvellous experience of Christ's kingdom in heaven. Some churches do still teach the absurd doctrine that only members of *that* church will finish up in the church triumphant. Although officially some churches still teach this nonsense, only a handful pay it any more than lip service. We find it difficult to believe that going to church on Saturday or belief in Mary's sinlessness or pre-millenialism or any other -ism could be essential to the process of getting into heaven. Jesus' parable of the wheat and the weeds shows us what we have always known: that in the churches we have wheat and weeds, genuine Christians and hypocrites. And that's true of *all* the churches. But Jane's church, *the* church, is made up of *all* the Christians from *all* the churches in *all* the world and through *all* of history.

Then why do we have denominations? Why not just one church in each town? Well, ask yourself why you attend your church? Why not a different church? Well . . . I like the minister, and it's reasonably near home, and my friends go there, or my parents go there, or it has a good choir, or whatever. It's often got very little to do with *doctrine*. In fact most of us don't really know what the doctrine of the other churches is. Some years ago, I wrote an article in the *British Weekly* suggesting that most Baptists don't know why they aren't Methodists and Methodists don't know why they aren't Anglicans. The following week there was an irate reply. From a man. He most certainly *did* know why he was Brethren and not Baptist, and he proceeded to list (I think) ten reasons. The funny thing was: in every one of the ten he had misunderstood what Baptists believe!

So there *is* one church. But many churches, because people like to worship God in different ways. A church doesn't need a special building to meet in, but it's convenient to have somewhere to meet regularly. So a building may be useful. Although very few churches make proper use of their buildings. Open on Sunday and closed all day Monday. With all the cost of overheads it might be wiser to think of house meetings or rented rooms in the community centre rather than building and maintaining a mausoleum. Which is what some churches look like. And feel like on a typical January Sunday morning!

One big problem that churches have is that too few people are doing too much of the work. Now the church is like a body, so Paul tells us. For a healthy body all the parts need exercise. But the church sometimes looks suspiciously like a body with all mouth and no hands or feet. Or if the hands and feet are there they have gone to sleep. And unfortunately if a visiting preacher or a new minister wakes them up a bit they get pins and needles. That's uncomfortable. They'd rather sleep, thank you. So out goes the new idea or the new minister. But that sleep is the sleep of death. It's a sick sleep. And if we have one sick member then we all need to look at our bill of health. Sickness in the church is catching.

So we do need churches, groups of people, and we do need somewhere for them to meet, although a big building could be a hindrance.

Do we need ministers? Well . . . yes. But ministers simply

must learn what they *can* do and what they *can't* do, and stop trying to be everything from the Chairman of the Laundry Sub-Committee to Song Leader, Preacher, Editor, Scholar, Sick Visitor and Counsellor (the capital letters are intentional: that's how we think of these jobs) all rolled into one. When the minister functions as a general factotum he accomplishes two things: he makes it impossible for himself to do what he *is* qualified for and he prevents other people in the church from doing what *they* are qualified for.

But worth-while teaching takes a lot of preparation. It doesn't get knocked up in half an hour on Saturday night. So churches may need to pay ministers so that they can give time to studying the Bible and planning worth-while teaching. In spite of the fashion for 'discussion groups' (you bring your ignorance and I'll bring mine, and somehow by putting zero to zero we'll come up with some positive score) there's no substitute for proper teaching.

I think that it was G. K. Chesterton's father who told him, when he was a boy, that if he would only put away a shilling a week, he would be surprised at what it would add up to over a year. As Chesterton pithily remarked, he would have been very surprised indeed if it had added up to anything other than fifty-two shillings! The laws of arithmetic are inexorable whether applied to savings or sermons: you get out what you put in.

The church. Divided. With many divisions, many members, but still, one church. Not visibly one. Not, I suspect, capable of being crammed into one outward form. But for all that, under Christ's headship, *one*. You are *in* the church.

THINK IT OVER

1. Find someone from another denomination to come and talk about his church. Try to read something about his church. During your talks try to spot when you get uncomfortable. When you feel smug. After the session write down what you have learned about the other church.

2. Read Ephesians, 4.1–6. These few verses talk about the one-ness of the Spirit, the bond of peace, the one body, one Spirit, one hope, one Lord, one faith, one baptism and one God. A life worthy of the Lord seems to mean taking all this unity seriously: more seriously than most of us do. Why do you think that unity discussed in committees never seems to work out in anything practical? Can you think of examples of unity in action? What steps has your church taken recently to work with or pray with or study with other churches?

3. Where does unity have to stop?

4. What *is* a Christian? No, not 'What does a Christian have to believe?' but simply . . . What *is* a Christian?

CHAPTER 4

One Way

One of the great Christian virtues is humility. But on one subject the Christian seems to be arrogant, stubborn, unreasonable, inflexible, uncompromising. He insists: there's only one way to God and that's through Jesus.

He won't allow philosophers to speculate about God's nature. He won't learn from the teachings of other religions about God. He won't put their religious books along with his Bible. For the Christian it's one way: Jesus' way.

The temptation to compromise is strong. Most other religions are prepared to be humble about their claims. Islam accepts the virgin birth of Jesus and makes Jesus one of the great prophets and even expects him to come back again. Hinduism will welcome Jesus into the ranks of its great Gurus. Even Judaism is looking again at Jesus' claims to be Messiah (although not at all ready to see Jesus as God's Son). But when other religions hold out the hand of tolerance and friendship, the supposedly humble and meek followers of Jesus ignore it. They'll not take one step away from the uncompromising *one way*.

Of course, some Christians have succumbed to the pressure to think again. It means dropping the idea of the total authority of the Bible. It means allowing man to search for God, and then to find him . . . or at least to get a glimpse of him. But inevitably that first step is like pulling out the keystone of the arch: suddenly everything caves in.

WHAT THE BIBLE SAYS

Acts 4.7–12
(Peter and John had healed a lame man, by calling on the

name of Jesus. A crowd gathered and they were arrested. The next day the Council interrogated them):

So the two disciples were brought in before them.

'By what power, or by whose authority have you done this?' the Council demanded.

Then Peter, filled with the Holy Spirit, said to them, 'Honourable leaders and elders of our nation, if you mean the good deed done to the cripple, and how he was healed, let me clearly state to you and to all the people of Israel that it was done in the name and power of Jesus from Nazareth, the Messiah, the man you crucified – but God raised him back to life again. It is by his authority that this man stands here healed! For Jesus the Messiah is . . . a "stone discarded by the builders which became the capstone of the arch".

'There is salvation in no one else! Under all heaven there is no other name for men to call upon to save them.'

John 14.1–6

(Or read the words of Jesus: he said the same thing, and no doubt that's where the disciples got their teaching from):

'Let not your heart be troubled. You are trusting God, now trust in me. There are many homes up there where my Father lives, and I am going to prepare them for your coming. When everything is ready, then I will come and get you, so that you can always be with me where I am. If this weren't so, I would tell you plainly. And you know where I am going and how to get there.'

'No, we don't,' Thomas said. 'We haven't any idea where you are going, so how can we know the way?'

Jesus told him, 'I am the Way – yes, and the Truth, and the Life. No one can get to the Father except by means of me.'

THINKING IT THROUGH

But surely all religions point to God? Well, just stop a minute while we do a little grammar because that statement, 'all religions point to God' contains a great big grammatical trap. So grammar first.

There are two kinds of nouns, *proper nouns* and *common nouns*. 'Peter' is a proper noun, that's me. But I am a 'man'. That's a common noun, because there are lots of men, all different. 'Table' is a common noun because there are lots of tables, and 'carpenter' is a common noun because there are lots of carpenters making lots of tables. Even the word 'king' is a common noun because there have been lots of kings although there aren't too many around just now. What about the word 'god'? You're right! I've made a change: we're talking about god and not about God-with-a-capital-G. The word 'god' is a common noun. There are many gods, the Hindu Shiva or Vishnu, the African Yembe or Waqa, Ahura Mazda of the Zoroastrians and all the rest. But the Bible insists: there is only one God.

Now we can see what the catch is in that little sentence: 'All religions lead to God.' Who is this particular god we are talking about? Do all religions lead to the terrible Shiva? Did the Father of Jesus command us to kill our enemies wherever we find them? Shiva is described in the Hindu Vedas, their scriptures, as a grotesque and horrible monster. Muhammad believed that Allah commanded his followers to kill their enemies. Are these gods all the same person? Are they all God?

That little sentence plays a trick with logic. A little like the game we used to play:

'I can prove that you aren't here.'
'All right, prove it!'
'Well, are you in Birmingham?'
'No.'
'Are you in Paris?'
'No.'
'Are you in Brazil?'
'No.'
'Well then, if you're not in Birmingham, and you're not in Paris and you're not in Brazil, then you must be somewhere else . . . and if you're somewhere else you can't be here!'

But 'somewhere else' means 'somewhere other than Birmingham, Paris and Brazil', not 'somewhere else, other than *here*'.

Or that little sentence makes the same mistake as I would if I argued:

'I have a table and you have a table, therefore, you have my table.'

You see, 'table' is a common noun, not a proper noun.

Actually, it is obviously absurd to suggest that all religions are really the same. How can they be? The key to Confucius and his philosophy is that man is basically good. The key to Christianity is that man is basically bad. Christianity says that the individual is vitally important; Buddhism teaches that the individual doesn't really exist at all. Hinduism says that the universe has no beginning, but Christianity says that God created it. The Jains are not allowed to eat anything that has life, while the Christian is told that he can eat any kind of meat, while again the Muslim can't eat pork and the Australian aborigine may be forbidden to eat kangaroo. Christianity says that Christ died on a cross for our sins, the Muslim denies that he died on the cross at all.

Why don't *we* have a *proper* name for God, like the Hindus or the Zoroastrians? Well, we have one. God actually revealed his name to Moses. We used to spell it *Jehovah* but probably it ought to be spelled out as *Yahweh*. But we don't use that name. The reason is that the Jews felt that this name was too holy for ordinary people to make use of it, so instead of reading the name Yahweh they always read 'Lord'. So then we can make this problem of the one way clear by asking: is Yahweh the same as Shiva? Is Shiva the same as Ahura Mazda? And the answer has to be No! Because God can't contradict himself and say one thing in 1300 BC to Moses, then something different to Zoroaster in 600 BC, change his mind again when talking to Paul in AD 60 and say something quite different again to Muhammad in AD 610. *We* can change *our* minds but we can hardly trust in a god who does the same.

There *is* only one God. But there are many gods. The gods are not God. God has revealed himself in his Son, Jesus Christ our Lord. So when people tell us, 'Of course I believe in god', we respond: 'Which god do you believe in? Is he "the God and Father of our Lord Jesus Christ"?' (That's 2 Corinthians 1.3 and 11.31). If he isn't, then although he may be that person's god, he is not God.

God-with-a-capital-G is 'The God and Father of our Lord Jesus Christ.' The God of our Lord Jesus Christ because he is the God who was revealed by, described by, Jesus. The other title, 'Father' is a reminder of God's special relationship to Jesus. God is the Father of us all. But we are born with a human father and a human mother. Jesus wasn't. Joseph didn't decide when Jesus should be born. God the Father did. Jesus' birth was a Trinitarian affair. The Father sent the Son through the Holy Spirit. It was entirely God's idea, God's plan. Not man's. And particularly not Joseph's. When we speak about God, we mean the God who was revealed by Jesus and we mean the God who sent Jesus into the world.

So, when someone tells me, 'Of course I believe in god', I make a mental note that 'god' is a common noun. I now have to find out which god he believes in. Is it Allah, or Vishnu or Ahura Mazda, or Diana, the goddess of hunting, or some nature god or who? Or is he actually talking about God? The one God?

All roads lead to heaven

Well, I'm just a bloke from London
    and I know that I'm no saint,
I'm a sinner and I knows it,
    I'm no hypocrite I ain't.
So I went to see the vicar and
    I asked him what to do
And his answer might have come
    straight from the monkeys at the zoo:
    'There isn't any cause to fret, between just me and you
    all roads lead at last to heaven like all lead to Timbuktu.'

Well, I'm just a bloke from London
    and I know I ain't no brain.
I'm the driver of the bus from
    Waterloo to Petticoat Lane.

And of one thing I'm quite certain.
　　When I drive the number seven
And I aim for Waterloo
　　I don't expect to get to heaven!
　　Well the passengers might grumble and they might kick
　　　　up a fuss
　　if they find the angel Gabriel a-riding on me bus!

Or, suppose some bloke should ask me:
　　'Which way, mate, for Camden Town?'
And I said, 'Go north, or east, or south,
　　or west, or up or down.
'Cos it don't make any difference,
　　all roads go to Timbuktu.
All roads go to Camden Town
　　and all roads lead to heaven, too.'
　　I can guess what 'e would say, I haven't got the slightest
　　　　doubt.
　　' 'ere mates, this bloke is drunk, or daft, 'e's balmy', 'e
　　　　would shout.

Well, I'm just a bloke from London,
　　and I know I ain't so bright
And the vicar's bin to college
　　and 'e should know wrong from right.
He should know the road to heaven
　　like I do to Waterloo,
'Cos if all roads lead to heaven
　　and all go to Timbuktu,
　　Maybe all roads lead to nowhere and for all that I can tell
　　All those roads *don't* lead to heaven ... maybe all roads
　　　　lead to hell?

Only one way. It really isn't on to suggest that all religions
are the same at heart, because they all seek after 'god'. Try
telling a Communist that his beliefs are the same as a Tory's
really: after all they are both political parties. Or that a
whale is the same as a giraffe because they're both
mammals. Or try advertising steaks and handing out saus-

What it says about . . .	HINDUISM	BUDDHISM	ISLAM	CHRISTIANITY
God	Many gods: Vishnu, Brahma and Shiva emerged as most important	God is beyond our knowledge and not our concern	There is one god, Allah (means 'The' god)	A Trinity, Father, Son and Spirit, in Unity
Scriptures	A huge collection of books, with the Vedas, as most important, in Sanskrit	The Ti-pitaka or 'Three Baskets', in the Pali language	The Qur'an, in Arabic	The Old and New Testaments written in Hebrew and Greek
The world	Uncreated, eternal: cyclic, in repeated periods called Days of Brahman	The material world is an illusion	Created by Allah in six days	Created by God
Heaven	No heaven, except in popular Hinduism	Nirvana is the goal, not heaven	A sensual sort of heaven	A spiritual concept with no marriage, no pain
Salvation	Through knowledge of the truth about his identity with Brahman	Through eliminating all desires: the middle way	Through submission to Allah and observation of the five 'Pillars'	Through faith in and obedience to Christ
Behaviour	Do what is expected of your caste	Avoid all extremes, of asceticism or of luxury	Follow the example of Muhammad; obey Qur'an and Tradition	Follow the example of Christ and obey His word.

ages because they're both meat! The world's religions are all different . . . and there's just one that leads us to God.

THINK IT OVER

1. What *is* 'religion'? Look up the dictionary definition. What does religion try to do? Is there such a thing as religion without god? Or without *a* god of some sort?

2. Jesus said, 'I am the way.' Can you think of some *other* way for us to find God? Gautama is called Buddha, or 'enlightened one' because he sat under a tree, thinking about the mystery of life until at last he worked out the secret of life. Basically he said, 'Life is made miserable because of so much suffering. Suffering comes because we want things. If we can only stop wanting things then suffering will stop. And you can stop wanting things if you will just learn to control your thoughts and actions. When you learn to do that you will be able to escape from rebirth into the world.'

There are five sentences there, each with one statement in it. Discuss those five statements. How true are they? Is all suffering, all pain, bad? Is toothache bad? Or does it have a helpful side to it? What's the trouble with Gautama's solution, 'learn to control your thinking and your actions'?

3. In Galatians 3.11 Paul writes: '. . . it is clear that no one can ever win God's favour by trying to keep the Jewish laws, because God has said that the only way we can be right in his sight is by faith.'

What is faith? What is the connection between faith and obedience? (look at John 14, verses 15 to the end of the chapter).

CHAPTER 5

Never Mind the Rules

There are two kinds of rules: rules of deduction and rules of convention.

The first kind, rules of deduction, are there to be found. They are part of the world. They can't be changed by us. Our job is to discover what these rules are and to try to express them as clearly as we can.

The law of gravity is a rule which applies to everything material in the universe. Rather crudely we may explain the law by saying that if you let go of any heavy object it will fall to the ground. More carefully, we may say that the earth is attracted towards the heavy object and moves towards it, while the heavy object is attracted towards the earth and moves towards *it*. Because the earth is so much 'heavier' than our object we can't detect its movement at all and because our object, however heavy, is still light compared to the earth we see it 'fall'. More carefully still we might deal with the law of gravity in terms of Einstein and his theory of relativity. These three views of the law of gravity don't have any effect at all on the law. It is just there. It can't be changed although we may find out new facts about the law.

Rules of deduction, like the rules concerning gravity, apply to everyone. These rules don't have to be believed in. They are simply *there*. When a child drops his toys out of the pram, gravity doesn't stop to consider whether he is old enough to understand the law of gravity. When a child puts his hand into the fire there is no pause to find out whether or not the child's parents have warned him of the effect of fire. The child is burned . . . the law is inexorable.

Rules of convention are different, although some rules of convention do seem to be 'built in' to the world. Most countries have a rule about murder, although they all seem to agree that the rule is suspended under certain conditions in war time. Rules about stealing, also, seem to be fairly universal, although some countries' policies of 'nationalisation' without paying any compensation would look very much like stealing if carried out by me or you, instead of by a government.

Rules of convention also apply to things like eating. In some homes dinner would begin with soup, then on to fish, next a joint, some kind of sweet and finally coffee. Nothing very terrible would happen if the process were reversed, starting with coffee and finishing with soup. It would probably result in some raised eyebrows amongst the guests, but it wouldn't be an *immoral* meal and no one would be punished either for serving it or for eating it.

On the other hand if society decided that murderers should no longer be dealt with in *some* way the consequences would be rather serious.

If there is a rule of any kind, careful observation should show us the consequences of the rule itself and of breaking the rule. The rule about dinner would be tested by entering a few thousand homes to see how dinner was served. The consequence of breaking the rule would consist of the raised eyebrows and possibly the determination of guests never to go there for dinner again.

Now this is all right for rules of convention. And partly right for rules of deduction. But rules of deduction *can not be broken*. The man who declared that he didn't believe in the law of gravity and jumped off Beachy Head to prove his point didn't break the law of gravity. He broke his neck.

In fact, when a law of deduction appears to be broken we at once suspect that something is wrong: either with our facts or with our understanding of the law. For example, the discovery of the planet Pluto followed a study of the orbits of the other planets around the sun. They didn't seem to be quite in keeping with the laws governing gravity. Either the rules were wrong, or something had been left out of the calculations. Pluto had been left out ... 3,600 million miles out in space.

So here is a difference between rules of deduction and

rules of convention. Rules of convention can be broken. Rules of deduction can't. But rules of convention have attached to them *consequences*. If you break the rules certain consequences follow. You go to prison, you pay a fine, you lose your dinner guests, you lose your friends or you might even lose your job.

Language, too, has its rules. We talk about *one* house and *two* houses, where the Germans use *ein* and *zwei* while in Ethiopia they speak of *and* and *hulet*. There's no real reason why we shouldn't change things around and count *one, three, two* if we want to . . .

* * *

For this sketch you need four players, although the two medical attendants don't speak. Andrew's part is straightforward. But George will need to practise his part because what he has to say is contrary to the speech habits that he has acquired. Many of our word sequences, plus their associated actions (pointing upwards, nodding, stamping the foot) are fixed, rather like loops of tape in our minds. We start the tape playing and it's very difficult to change any part of what we are going to say. That's why most preachers have meaningless phrases which pop out predictably right through their sermons: '. . . the nurture and admonition of the Lord', 'the first day of another week', 'bless and sanctify', 'travelling through this wilderness scene' are all phrases that I remember belonging to particular preachers. George has some of these loops. He is going to break the loops. And it's not easy. For example, he will find it very difficult to say 'three times six is twelve' and even more difficult to say:

'You mean the floor down there?' while he points to the ceiling.

ANDREW: Hi!
GEORGE: Hi! . . . Someone said you were looking for me.
ANDREW: Well . . . I wanted to talk to you a bit. Are you the guy who has his arithmetic all mixed up?
GEORGE: (*takes offence*) What do you mean, my arithmetic

all mixed up? There's nothing wrong with my arithmetic. It's different, that's all.

ANDREW: Well, I don't know. The other guys say that you add one and one and get *three*.

GEORGE: So? One and one *do* make three.

ANDREW: Uh, uh! One and one make *two*. See, let me show you . . . (*holds up fingers and counts*) One (*sticks up one finger*) and one (*sticks up another finger*) makes (*counts*) one, *two*.

GEORGE: Well, of course, if you count that way. But that's not right. See . . . one (*sticks up one finger*) and one (*sticks up a second finger*), make . . . (*counts*) one, *three*.

ANDREW: One, three! Good night! Who taught you to count, the Inland Revenue?
(*writes on the blackboard:*

    1   *one*
    2   *two*
    3   *three*

and then reads aloud)
See, one, two, three.

GEORGE: That's sort of weird. Look: (he *writes on blackboard:*

    1   one
    2   *three*
    3   *two*

and then reads aloud)
One, three, two.

ANDREW: Oh no! Say . . . what's three times six?

GEORGE: Three times six? Twelve.

ANDREW: Three times six is twelve! Wait a minute. Here, let me write it down
(*writes on the blackboard* 3×6)

GEORGE: If you mean two times six why don't you say so? Two times six is eighteen.

ANDREW: Two times six is eighteen and three times six is twelve! Look . . . do you know your Bible? John three sixteen, for example?

GEORGE: John three sixteen . . . that's a bit unusual isn't it? Something about the cleansing of the Temple . . . 'take these things hence and do not make my Father's house into a market . . .'

ANDREW: Eeeek! That's John *two* sixteen!

GEORGE: Oh no . . . John *two* sixteen is the famous verse, 'For God so loved the world . . .'

ANDREW: Look . . . could you write that on the blackboard? John three sixteen, I mean.

GEORGE: On the white board?

ANDREW: White board? *White* board he says! (*sudden thought*) Here . . . what colour's this chalk?

GEORGE: (*matter of fact*) Black.

ANDREW: (*desperate*) Well . . . what colour is the ceiling up there? (*points upwards*)

GEORGE: (*also points up*) You mean the colour of the floor down there?

ANDREW: The floor down there!! (*points down*) The floor down there is dark brown boards.

GEORGE: Not at all . . . (*points down*) The ceiling up there is almost white . . . (*points up*) but the floor down there is black!

ANDREW: (*recaps*) One, three, two . . .
Three times six is twelve and two times six is eighteen.
John three sixteen is John two sixteen.
Blackboards are whiteboards, up is down,
and the ceiling is black down there.
Wow! (*Blows his whistle; the two attendants come in and proceed to grab George and carry him off, struggling*) He communicates! He really does communicate! And the message I get is that he's crazy . . . or I am. Take him away! (*exit*)

WHAT THE BIBLE SAYS

Romans 7.7–12

I would never have known the sin in my heart – the evil desires that are hidden there – if the law had not said, 'You must not have evil desires in your heart.' But sin used this law against evil desires by reminding me that such desires are wrong and arousing all kinds of forbidden desires within me! Only if there were no laws to break would there be no sinning.

That is why I felt fine so long as I did not understand what the law really demanded. But when I learned the truth, I realised that I had broken the law and was a sinner, doomed to die. So far as I was concerned, the good law which was supposed to show me the way of life resulted instead in my being given the death penalty. Sin fooled me by taking the good laws of God and using them to make me guilty of death. But still, you see, the law itself was wholly right and good.

2 Timothy 2.5
Follow the Lord's rules for doing his work, just as an athlete either follows the rules or is disqualified and wins no prize.

Exodus 22.1–3
If a man steals an ox or sheep and then kills or sells it, he shall pay a fine of five to one – five oxen shall be returned for each stolen ox. For sheep, the fine shall be four to one – four sheep returned for each sheep stolen.

If a thief is caught in the act of breaking into a house and is killed, the one who killed him is not guilty. But if it happens in the daylight, it must be presumed to be murder, and the man who kills him is guilty.

If a thief is captured, he must make full restitution; if he can't, then he must be sold as a slave for his debt.

John 14.15
If you love me, obey me.

FREE FROM THE LAW

Free from the Law, Oh, happy condition,
I can sin as I like and still have remission!

Well, you can't. Sin as you like, that is. This matter of freedom seems to cause people so much trouble and mostly it's because we think far too much about our rights. Now we *are* free from the Old Testament Law. We must be, because that Law had three parts to it:

1. The Law itself
2. The blessings that would follow if the Law was obeyed
3. The consequences that would follow if the Law was *not* obeyed.

I don't have any doubt about our freedom from the Old Testament Law given to Moses. Otherwise we really ought to be still putting out our fires on Friday afternoon and sacrificing lambs. Because of Leviticus 19.19 we would have to think very carefully about planting carrots and cabbages in the same field. But we *are* free from those laws. It's just as well that we are free from them because we couldn't obey them anyway! We were enslaved by sin. We sinned not because we particularly *wanted* to, but because we couldn't help ourselves. Paul's own experience is the same as ours:

> I don't understand myself at all, for I really want to do what is right, but I can't. I do what I don't want to do – what I hate. I know perfectly well that what I am doing is wrong, and my bad conscience proves that I agree with these laws I am breaking. But I can't help myself, because I'm no longer doing it. It is sin inside me that is stronger than I am that makes me do these evil things. (Romans 7.15–17)

The Law doesn't help us to behave. In fact it does the opposite. It still does! Put up a notice saying 'don't touch' and people who didn't want to touch before will find the most extraordinary urge to touch now. Tell a child not to sit in that chair and he will at once experience an irresistible desire to sit there.

The Grace of God frees us from this captivity to sin. We

don't *have* to sin. At the same time, grace frees us from the Old Testament Law because that Law involved punishment for those who don't keep it. BUT. BUT.

The Grace of God did not make us lawless.

We are free. Not free to please ourselves, but for the first time *free to serve God.*

Paul again expressed it so simply: 'Now you are free from the power of sin and are *slaves of God.*' (Romans 6.22)

Actually the church at Corinth had a problem with this matter of keeping the Law. They realised that they were free from sin. So they assumed that they were free from the Old Testament Law. All right. And that they were free from all law. All wrong. There *are* laws governing the Christian life:

'Follow the Lord's rules for doing his work, just as an athlete either follows the rules or is disqualified and wins no prize.' (2 Timothy 2.5)

Now try to follow this carefully. The Christians at Corinth had a difficult problem. The slaughterhouses, where the cows were butchered, were all attached to pagan temples. And when a cow had its throat cut it was dedicated to the 'god' of the temple. People who worshipped *that* god ate *that* meat. But, of course, there was no Christian temple and so no 'Christian' meat. The Christians argued like this:

'We are intelligent people. We have been saved from devils and superstition. We know that these idols are just bits of wood. They most certainly aren't God. We have no need to fear them. So let's feel free to buy our meat where we like and even eat it in the Temple café if we want to.'

Other Christians weren't so sure. If the gods weren't gods then what were they? They weren't *nothing.* There was something devilish about them. So they decided that they ought not to go in the temples at all. They'd simply have to manage without the Sunday joint.

But then they got a shock. As they walked past the Temple cafés they saw Christians in them. Cheerfully eating meat!

'Come on in! It's all right! No need for us to fear these so-called gods. There's nothing to it. We're free from all that superstition.'

'Well . . .'

And some walked on because they weren't convinced and some walked in even though they weren't convinced and some walked in because they were convinced. Those who were in already didn't come to any harm. Those who walked on didn't come to any harm. Those who were convinced didn't come to any harm. But those who weren't convinced, but went in anyway . . . . they had a bad night. Couldn't sleep. Worrying about what they'd done. *Was* it all right? Sitting in a place like that? And the things that went on there . . . the Temple prostitutes hanging around . . . one felt so *dirty* even sitting there . . . And that was just the first of a whole lot of sleepless nights. Worrying.

Back to the Christians who went in first of all. Were they all right? Well . . . they were right in thinking that they no longer needed to fear the gods or demons or whatever of the temples. But. They forgot. We all have a responsibility for other people. And because of that some things which would be perfectly safe and proper for us have to go. What those things are will differ from country to country. It's unlikely to mean no roast beef. But Paul was quite ready even for that:

'So, if eating meat offered to idols is going to make my brother sin, I'll not eat any of it as long as I live.' (1 Corinthians 8.13)

We are free from the Old Testament Law, but we are not left lawless. Jesus commanded us to love God with all our hearts, and to love our neighbours as we love ourselves. And that's not the only commandment he gave. There are dozens of them in the New Testament:

children are to obey their parents

husbands are to love their wives

we are not to lie to each other

we are to make disciples of all nations

we are to pray without ceasing

and there are plenty more to find.

There's a real danger around today when Christians shout about their freedom. Liberation! Yes! Set free . . . to serve God.

THINK IT OVER

1. Collect fifty New Testament commandments. What happens if we obey them? What happens if we don't obey them?

2. Is it fair to apply the thinking behind the question of eating meat offered to idols to drinking in a pub? I don't drink any alcohol. Why not? After all, Jesus turned water into the best wine! (I wonder if in these days he might have made coffee for them?)

CHAPTER 6

And They All Lived Happily Ever After

Well, they didn't. They had their problems. Because living the Christian life is hard, hard, hard.

But there are still so many Christians who haven't got hold of this fundamental fact: living the Christian life is hard, hard, hard. Some preachers encourage us to believe that once you've got over the hurdle of conversion, becoming a Christian, everything else is easy.

You marry a marvellous guy.

You get a stupendous job . . .

and then get promoted right over the heads of sixteen others who are really senior to you (but, poor fish, are not *real* Christians).

You buy a nice house at least four hundred pounds under market price.

Your children pass their examinations and all become Christians, and if you happen to get sick, well, a word of prayer and a miraculous recovery without any penicillin at all.

And of course, business prospers. Especially if you tithe:

'When I started this business I decided that I was going to give the Lord a tenth of all the profits. Well, of course I was tempted a few times, when things went badly, but I stuck to it and God always had his tenth. The business picked up. So I gave the Lord a fifth. That came to a lot of money, but God is no man's debtor and profits just kept going right on up. Now God gets a quarter of all the profits and . . .'

Now there's a measure of truth in all this. God does often miraculously provide for us. There are the Peters who are

58

miraculously released from prison. But we tend to forget the Jameses and the John-the-Baptists who don't get released. I shall never forget the plaque on the wall of a London hospital:

In loving memory
Dr and Mrs Ian Sharpe,
Jillian, Alison and Andrew
Who laid down their lives for Christ
in the Congo
November 25 1964

Having been a missionary myself, and having my own little family, I have often pictured the events lying behind that simple plaque.

Living the Christian life is hard, hard, hard.

It's a very different thing from playing at church. It's Sister Teresa amongst the outcasts of Calcutta, and my own special saint, Sister Gabriel, who used to live amongst the burnt-out sufferers from leprosy in the graveyards of Addis Ababa. What a saint she was! Roman Catholic. But when I met her we were just one in the Lord. She was working in a lonely spot with a young priest. She was white-haired, old enough to be his grandmother. I was amused to see how respectfully she addressed him as 'Father'. With a twinkle in her eye. Because the real saints always seem to have a sense of humour . . .

But while the Christian life *is* hard, we often *make* it hard for ourselves, by refusing to live out in our lives what we know in our hearts: that God loves us. That the hard, hard experiences of our lives are not the result of 'bad luck', nor are they God reaching down to punish us for our sins. Of course some sins *are* followed by retribution. But when things go wrong in our lives we begin to look around and to ask . . . Why?

And someone, somewhere, is sure to see the wrath of God in it.

*　　　*　　　*

Anne is a Christian. Thirty-ish, distraught. Her husband has been involved in a car smash, and is in hospital. She finds it hard to cope with the situation. Her finances are strained. She has a troubled conscience, but she isn't quite ready to talk about that . . . not yet.

She is a Christian, yes, but most of the time she manages to rub along pretty well without God. She doesn't know too much about him, although she has picked up some ideas along the way. Anne is praying . . .

ANNE: (*she sounds taut, desperate*) God? . . . are you there? Can I talk to you?

(*to herself*) I wish he would say something . . . God? . . . I'm in a mess . . . Can't you see? Don't you care? Please . . . God?

GOD: I'm here. I'm always here. And when you seek me with all your heart you will always find me. I am always with you . . . but you are not always with me. What do you want?

ANNE: You're God! You know already!

GOD: I want you to tell me.

ANNE: Oh . . . what's the use . . . you wouldn't understand.

GOD: I was born in a cowshed, I worked with my hands, I walked and I wept, I was hungry, tired and thirsty. I was betrayed by my friends, laughed at by my enemies and put to death on a cross. What wouldn't I understand?

ANNE: (*blurts it out*) All right . . . I'll tell you. It's Pete. He's in hospital. Because of the car smash. But that's not all. It's money. You see we bought the new car . . . and we had to pay for the tax on it, and insurance . . . and we had some new furniture . . . and clothes . . . and we've been going out an awful lot . . . and I've overspent . . . (*pause*)

GOD: (*waits, and then*) . . . Is that all?

ANNE: (*a little sulkily*) No. You know the other thing.

GOD: I want you to tell me.

ANNE: It's that hundred pounds isn't it? I saw it lying on the floor in the supermarket just by the cash desk. I've never even seen a hundred-pound note before. I whipped it up . . . nobody saw me . . .

GOD: (*interrupts, sharply*) I saw you.

ANNE: (*pause, then*) Nobody except you . . . (*wildly*) And now the car's smashed up and Pete's in hospital, and I'll never be able to pay all the bills and get the car fixed up and everything . . . I suppose it's all a judgement on me for stealing that money . . .

GOD: Do you really think that's how I work? Smashing up your car and putting your husband in hospital just to pay you back for petty theft? Where do you get these ideas about me?

ANNE: (*matter-of-fact*) From the Bible, I suppose. (*fiercely*) Don't you bring judgement on children's children to the third and fourth generation?

GOD: I show mercy to those who love me.

ANNE: (*flatly*) I don't think that I believe in love any more. What *is* love?

GOD: I am love. I sent my Son to you because I love you. We understand how you feel. But don't blame me for Pete's accident. The other driver had just had a row with his wife. Had a drink to calm himself down. He wasn't driving too well . . . He needs me, too, just now. He's afraid that your husband might die.

ANNE: Oh God . . . what a mess . . . (*pause*) Can you help us at all? Will you? . . . Maybe if I . . .

GOD: (*interrupts, sharply*) You can't bargain with me.

ANNE: No. (*pause*) But I can't keep it . . . the money I mean. Every time I open my purse it's there . . . glaring at me . . . (*makes up her mind*) I don't care what happens . . . I'm taking it back.

GOD: I *can* help you . . .

WHAT THE BIBLE SAYS

Psalm 69.1–3 (RSV)
> Save me, O God!
> For the waters have come up to my neck.
> I sink in deep mire, where there is no foothold;
> I have come into deep waters, and the flood sweeps over
>   me.

I am weary with my crying; my throat is parched.
My eyes grow dim with waiting for my God.

Deuteronomy 5.6–10 (RSV)
I am the Lord your God, who brought you out of the land of
  Egypt, out of the house of bondage.
You shall have no other gods before me.
You shall not make for yourself a graven image,
      or any likeness of anything that is in heaven above,
      or that is on the earth beneath,
      or that is in the water under the earth;
you shall not bow down to them or serve them;
for I the Lord your God am a jealous God, visiting the
  iniquity of the fathers upon the children to the third and
  fourth generation of those who hate me,
but showing steadfast love to thousands of those who love
      me and keep my commandments.

1 John 1.9 (RSV)
If we confess our sins, he is faithful and just, and will forgive
our sins.

THE THIRD LAW

Let's get one thing straight: God is just. But that doesn't
mean that he is sitting up there on a cloud, a hefty club in
one hand, waiting for us to make just one mistake so that he
can hand out mayhem. It should be obvious to us that
there's no one-to-one correspondence between our sins and
our crises. Our sins are too many for one thing! The world is
too complex, for another. Every action follows on from
thousands of others, and every action in its turn affects thousands of fresh actions.

Just imagine the effect that one person's smile can have on
the events of a day. Because the lady in the paper shop
smiled at George Robinson when he bought his usual *Mail*,
George, who is manager of a shoe shop, did not sack his
assistant, Judy, when she knocked a display stand filled with

seventy-five carefully arranged pairs of shoes into the middle of next week. So Judy did not break off her engagement to Bill when he turned up twenty minutes late for their date that night, and Bill . . . but you see what I mean.

Stealing-by-finding a hundred pounds ought to be enough to bother my conscience. Especially if shortly afterwards my husband has a nasty accident. But is that particular crime so very high on God's list of crimes? How can we possibly know what he considers to be trivial and what he considers to be fundamental. Taken at its face value, the biblical view of sin seems preposterous. To think adultery is equivalent to committing it. Getting angry is equivalent to murder.

But who am I to disagree with the biblical viewpoint? Just because I've thought adultery often enough, but never actually committed it. But if God's ideas about sin are so different from mine, I can't hope to produce any guaranteed hierarchy of sins. And if I can't do that then I can't hope to find any regular correspondence between my sins and God's supposed judgements.

When we take Psalm 69 seriously, we can see that it is precisely when things go wrong, when the water level reaches the neck, that we really begin our search for God. 'God shouts at us in our pains.' Even if we haven't talked with him for years, a real crisis can drive us to him in seconds. But then, when we do come to him like that, we have in the back of our minds a guilty remembrance of a frightening catalogue of sins, for any one of which God just might have decided to bring *this* on us.

The question of retribution, punishment for sin, has to be faced. The first fact to note is that every action does have some kind of result. Even cleaning my teeth in the morning. I clean my teeth in the morning and so just miss the bus (by the margin of time taken to clean my teeth) and the bus has an accident and I don't get hurt. I don't clean my teeth and what happens? Would I have been hurt if I had caught that bus? That I can never know, simply because my catching the bus would have changed the entire sequence of events. It would take a couple of seconds extra for me to get on the bus. That might avert the accident. My weight would make a slight difference to the speed of the bus, maybe just enough to avert the accident. Actually, if I had caught the bus the situation simply wouldn't have been the same at all.

I remember reading of an American pilot in the second world war. He was down to take part in an attack on an aircraft factory, deep inside Germany. The list of aircrews was put up, and as he stood there, reading the list, the Operations Officer erased his name from one crew and assigned him to another aircraft.

'He didn't know it, but that Operations Officer saved my life with a little piece of rubber.'

The plane to which he was originally assigned was shot down and all the crew was killed. Without that last minute change he would have been on that plane. He would have been killed.

But would he? In fact, if he had been on that plane everything about its flight would have been changed. The little piece of rubber on the end of a pencil certainly produced some changes, but we only know about some of the most obvious of those changes. As events worked out, one man lived, one man died, their children wept or their children were happy, and that effected *their* lives . . . probably to the third and fourth generations. But we simply can't say *why* one dies and another lives, why one suffers and another escapes suffering.

But I just don't believe that God organises a car smash to pay me back for petty theft. Have you ever seen a car smash? The sickly smell of blood mixed violently with the stench of petrol fumes, the white of protruding bones, the rasping breath of the casualties, the mute blankets over the humped forms of the dead? God doesn't *organise* that. He can take it into his purposes. But he doesn't arrange the accident.

There simply isn't any one-to-one correspondence between our sins and our crises. The book of Job ought to convince us of that. Job's friends all assumed that godliness and prosperity went together. So, when Job's farm was plundered and his family cut down and he was desperately ill, there was only one possible conclusion: he had done something terribly wrong and was concealing that fact. But God wouldn't let him get away with it.

Now the key to understanding the book of Job is the fact that Job himself is never given any explanation for his troubles. *We* get the explanation because we have the Prologue: the Tempter confidently asserting that Job served God only because it brought immunity from suffering, because it was a guarantee of success in business. God shows his confidence in Job, and refutes Satan's assertion, by allowing suffering into Job's life.

But notice that even so God doesn't *organise* Job's suffering. First of all he limits them: thus far and no further. And again, God takes Job's sufferings into his own purposes and gives *us* the whole story, to help us when things go wrong for us. We can know, from Job's sufferings, that not all suffering is retributive. Some suffering flows from carelessness, not caring. Some flows inevitably from the kind of society that we have created. Some follows from a refusal to lead the kind of life God has designed for us. And some suffering reflects another world altogether, the world of the Heavenlies, where the Accuser pits himself against God, and involves us in his warfare.

And yet ... and yet, while we have to recognise that we cannot find any one-to-one correspondence between my sins and my crises, we can still recognise the verdict of history: *in the long run* it is well with those who do well, and *in the long run* it is *not* well with those who do wrong.

But still on retribution. It is a dangerous undertaking to oppose God. You will have noticed that the retribution spoken of in Deuteronomy 5 is for those who *hate* God. Not merely live in ignorance of him, but positively, actively fight against him. To flout his standards, to laugh at his laws, to mock his demands, to deny his existence, to persecute his church, to ridicule his word ... these are serious undertakings indeed. The consequences of such conflicts with God may well be seen long past the third and fourth generations. But *hating* God is a far cry from the almost involuntary lapses of which we are all guilty.

And yet, sin does demand retribution. We feel this our-

-c

selves, intuitively. The Eichmann case makes it clear. As the story of Eichmann's vicious crimes against the Jews was told in court, all over the world people felt an almost helpless passion about it all. There was no adequate return for such cruelty. For him to die ... what was that? Justice seemed to demand so much more. The Christian teaching is that beyond our own human judgements there will always be God's own active judgement of sin. That judgement comes at two levels: the eternal and the here-and-now. Eternally, Jesus dealt with our sin. But if we persist in sin, if we *will* sin, there could well be a judgement on that sin here and now. Repented of, the sin can be forgiven and forgotten. Wilful sin is a different matter. If you won't ask for forgiveness then you can't be forgiven. Ananias and Sapphira, in Acts chapter 5 are a stunning example. Determined to make a name for themselves, they sold some land, tucked part of the proceeds away and then came to the church, pretending that they were now bringing the whole of the proceeds from the sale to be given to the church. What a sacrifice to offer! What generosity! What devotion to God! What an example to us all! What a sham! And what a death!

The Christian *is* involved in a conflict. There is the inner conflict, between the old nature and the newly awakened spirit. There is the external conflict, which is staged in the visible world, but which reflects the reality of the cosmic conflict between good and evil, between God and Satan. But this conflict, which we experience as individuals, affects us all. Each conflict we have with sin is like a stone thrown into a pond. The effects reach out and out to the very ends of the earth. The rubber on the end of a pencil can save lives and end lives, the smile can make a man and break a man ... and the effects of apparently trivial happenings reach out endlessly.

That is why we aren't allowed to please ourselves. Even the secular world won't let us please ourselves. If I want to drink and drive why shouldn't I? If I get killed, that's my business. Not so, says society, your drunken driving affects the Petes and the Annes of this world, the other drivers and the pedestrians.

God looks far deeper. Our conduct reflects the conflict in the world of the spirit. Our battle is ultimately one with the unseen world.

Now the strategy of this unseen world is flexible. C. S. Lewis, writing back in the 1940s, reflected on the Satanic strategy of his time. Screwtape is an Under-Secretary in one of Hell's Departments. Wormwood is a Junior Tempter:

My dear Wormwood,

I wonder you should ask me whether it is essential to keep the patient in ignorance of your own existence. That question, at least for the present phase of the struggle, has been answered for us by the High Command. Our policy, for the moment, is to conceal ourselves. Of course this has not always been so. We are really faced with a cruel dilemma. When the humans disbelieve in our existence we lose all the pleasing results of direct terrorism and we make no magicians. On the other hand, when they believe in us we cannot make them materialists and sceptics . . . I do not think that you will have much difficulty in keeping your patient in the dark. The fact that 'devils' are predominantly *comic* figures in the modern imagination will help you. If any faint suspicion of your existence begins to arise in his mind, suggest to him a picture of something in red tights, and persuade him that since he cannot believe in that, he therefore cannot believe in you . . .

Times have changed. While the devil still relies heavily on the absurd representation of cosmic powers dressed in red tights, horned and equipped with pitchforks, he has moved on to a new ploy. He is visible again. A sophisticated world that has failed to find any satisfaction in materialism has turned to spiritism. Witches and warlocks, wizards and necromancers, mediums and all their followers, openly practise their rites again. Oddly enough, this happens at a time when the developing countries have recognised and rejected the depressing, oppressing and repressing influence of the *shaman* or 'witch doctor'. But as the power of the *shaman* wanes in one world so it seems to wax in the West.

Following Jesus is not a pleasant afternoon stroll by the

river with a picnic to follow. It is much more than playing the guitar and singing soupy choruses. It is not sitting in a heavily upholstered seat in a centrally heated church listening to a titillating sermon. Following Jesus is potentially dangerous. It involves faith in God, obedience to Christ, conflict with Satanic powers. And the Christian life can be hard, hard, hard.

So. We can never hope to trace a one-to-one correspondence between our sins and our crises. Because there are too many sins. Because we don't know what God's scale of serious sins is. Because Christ died for our sins and the eternal aspect of retribution is already dealt with. Because the whole complex inter-relationship that is life is simply too complex. Because our visible warfare, as Christians, is a reflection of the spiritual warfare that goes on all the time. Because living the Christian life is hard, hard, hard.

The Third Law of Thermodynamics says that to every action there is an equal and opposite reaction. There's a kind of spiritual Third Law, too. Somewhere, some time, to every sin there has to be a divine reaction. We can't measure or predict that reaction. And God doesn't settle all accounts now. An old tract illustrates the point. A farmer had written to a local newspaper, boasting about his fields, but about one field in particular:

'I ploughed it on Sunday, I planted it on Sunday, I reaped it on Sunday and I threshed it on Sunday. And now, in September, I have a bigger harvest from that field than from any other of my fields.'

The editor had simply added the comment: 'God doesn't settle all his accounts in September.'

Actually, of course, if sin is anything even approaching the blasphemy the Bible pictures it as, then no car smash is ever going to deal with it. The two things are incommensurate. They don't fit. They are both appalling. They are both blotches on the universe. Each needs redress. And in the centre of history stands a cross which, in the mystery of God, deals *both* with my sin *and* my husband's car smash.

THINK IT OVER

1. What did Jesus mean when he said, 'Follow me!'? All Christians have been given the same command (Luke 9.23). What does this suggest to us about the Christian life?

2. Becoming a Christian doesn't provide us with an all-weather umbrella or an all-purpose insurance policy. Christians *do* share in the troubles experienced by the rest of the world. Why is that a *good* thing? Try to find at least ten good consequences.

3. What makes us think that Christians *ought* to be protected from the tragedies that hit other people? What is the mistake in this kind of thinking?

4. Christians can't expect to be sheltered from the troubles that everyone else goes through. How ought this to affect the way in which we pray for Christians who are in trouble? How do we usually pray for them?

CHAPTER 7

Telephone to Heaven

During a survey made in Germany people were asked about their belief in God and about their attitude to prayer. The results were interesting: 68 per cent of those interviewed said that they believed in God, but 86 per cent said that they prayed ... sometimes. Eighteen per cent of those people were doing a very odd kind of double-think, but this simply highlights the fact that prayer does not wait to be rational. I may say that I don't believe in God, but that need not prevent me from praying.

Personally I have no doubt that the most helpful book on prayer is a fairly old one: Harry Emerson Fosdick's *The Meaning of Prayer*. I would like to see just one more chapter added to this book: a chapter insisting that in prayer we have no need of a special language. Language is much more than words. Language includes the way in which words are strung together and the way in which the words are spoken: syntax and intonation. It is unfortunate that the church has developed both a special syntax and a special intonation for prayer.

It is said that Dean Inge used to take a book of theology into his stall to read during choral services. When asked to explain he said: 'During my life I have held many different views concerning the Creator, but it has never seemed to me likely that he would enjoy being serenaded!'

Possibly the Dean was being deliberately obtuse regarding the purpose of the choral service, but I certainly find it very difficult to imagine God's response to sung *prayers*. If they are still intended as prayers, that is. Praying is not the same as singing. Prayer is conversation with God. And the syntax and intonation of conversation are not the same as the syntax and intonation of singing. If prayer is conversation,

God ought to have the chance to reply. Does he have to sing his responses? If prayer is indeed conversation with God, what are we to make of operatic dialogue?

Prayer *is* conversation. God recognises our feeling of helplessness in this world. He offers to us the status of his children, and just as any family communicates, so this marvellous divine-human family communicates: through conversation. As children we talk *with*, not merely *to*, and certainly not *at*, God our Father.

However this picture reminds us that the relationship between child and father is not static, but dynamic. The relationship grows, deepens, changes. There is a great deal of difference between the almost total dependence on the father of a child of five and the dependence of the man of thirty-five. But it's not unmanly even for the man of thirty-five to ask his father for advice in an unfamiliar situation.

But his approach to his father will be different. The child of five brings his problem, dumps it into his father's hands and walks away, expecting his father to come up with a total solution. The man of thirty-five will already have some ideas as to how the problem might be solved. He might even want some explanation of those parts of the proposed solution which he finds hard to understand. But neither child nor man has any difficulty in approaching his father for advice.

Or perhaps he has.

Jesus once said to his followers: 'You men who are fathers – if your boy asks for bread, do you give him a stone? If he asks for fish, do you give him a snake? If he asks for an egg, do you give him a scorpion?'

Now Jesus didn't answer his question: he could assume that the answer was obvious. He could assume that fathers simply don't give snakes and scorpions to their children. Maybe we can't just assume that today. Maybe too many children of this generation have been handed snakes and scorpions by their fathers:

'What's wrong with smoking, son. There's nothing in the Bible against smoking,' and the habit of the cancer-stick has latched on like a lion on a gazelle's throat.

'What's wrong with the Pill, girl?' – and what ought to be a unique experience is devalued, debased for ever.

Perhaps some folks do have difficulty in thinking of God in terms of a Father who waits to give good gifts and only good gifts to his children. And maybe that does make conversation with him difficult.

WHAT THE BIBLE SAYS

Matthew 6.5–15
And now about prayer. When you pray, don't be like the hypocrites who pretend piety by praying publicly on street corners and in the synagogues where everyone can see them. Truly, that is all the reward they will ever get. But when you pray, go away by yourself, all alone, and shut the door behind you and pray to your Father secretly, and your Father, who knows your secrets, will reward you.

Don't recite the same prayer over and over as the heathen do, who think prayers are answered only by repeating them again and again. Remember, your Father knows exactly what you need even before you ask him.

Pray along these lines:

Our Father in heaven,
we honour your holy name.
We ask that your kingdom will come now;
May your will be done here on earth, just as it is in heaven.
Give us our food again today, as usual,
and forgive us our sins,
just as we have forgiven those who have sinned against us.
Don't bring us into temptation,
but deliver us from the Evil One.

Amen.

Your heavenly Father will forgive you, if you forgive those who sin against you; but if *you* refuse to forgive *them*, *he* will not forgive *you*.

Philippians 4.6
Don't worry about anything; instead, pray about everything; tell God your needs and don't forget to thank him for
his answers.

Acts 2.40–42
Then Peter preached a long sermon, telling about Jesus and
strongly urging all his listeners to save themselves from the
evils of their nation. And those who believed Peter were
baptised – about three thousand in all! They joined with the
other believers in regular attendance at the apostles' teaching sessions and at the Communion services and prayer
meetings.

PRAYING, POSTURING AND PUZZLING

Praying isn't 'doing what comes naturally'. Otherwise the
followers of Jesus wouldn't have come to him to ask him to
teach them how to do it. Again, praying is so important that
it's not surprising that it is also the most difficult discipline
of the Christian life. If that goes, the rest will follow.

When Jesus talked about prayer he made it clear that
praying can easily turn into posturing and pretending. We
may produce long prayers, we may produce eloquent
prayers, we may produce public prayers, but unless we
watch ourselves very carefully we will soon find that we have
stopped praying and started saying prayers. And there's a
heaven of difference between the two.

*   *   *

Jane again. She has progressed quite a way, the wrong way,
since we met her as a young Christian (p 33). She *has* joined
a church, and already she has picked up the church vocabu-
lary and the flowery rhetoric of her preacher. Fortunately
she still has her sense of humour and is not hopelessly jelled.

JANE: Our loving and gracious heavenly Father, Lord and
Creator of the universe, dwelling in light unapproachable
yet filled with mercy, Thou knowest . . .

73

GOD: Wait a minute, wait a minute. What *do* you think you're doing?

JANE: Huh? Lord? I'm praying. Like they do in our church. See, hands together, eyes closed. Our minister says that it's to shut out the world, the flesh and the devil. I've got the world switched off . . .

GOD: (*interrupts, drily*) . . . and your mind disengaged . . . What's all this 'Our loving heavenly Father, Thou knowest'?

JANE: (*flustered*) What? 'Our loving heavenly Father?' Well, they *always* start the prayer like that down at the church.

GOD: And you follow the tradition.

JANE: (*with spirit*) Well, after all, you taught . . . (*suddenly remembers*) oops! I mean Thou taughtest us that . . . Thou said . . . saidest . . . that we shouldest . . . should . . pray 'Our Father which art in heaven, hallowed be Thy name (*picks up speed with the familiar words*) Thy kingdom come, Thy will be done on earth as it is in heaven . . (*pauses for breath*). And Thou saidest . . . hath said . . .

GOD: Look, why can't you speak normally? You'll swallow your tongue if you try to twist it around all those Thees and Thous and thuses and saidests.

JANE: Oh . . . all right. Thank Thee . . . er . . . Thou . . .

GOD: (*prompts*) 'You.'

JANE: Thank you. (*pause, then blurts out*) But is it all right to call Thee 'you'? It sounds sort of familiar to me . . .

GOD: It's not really 'familiar' at all. In King James's day they used 'thee' and 'thou' when talking with their friends and they used 'you' when speaking to a stranger. Like the French *'tu'* and *'vous'*. In King James's time they knew me well enough to call me 'thee'. Nowadays you don't seem to know me well enough to call me 'you'!

JANE: (*a little deflated*) But . . . (*plucks up courage*) . . . thou art in heaven . . . I mean, you are in heaven, aren't you?

GOD: I am in heaven. I am also on earth. I am also right here, with you.

JANE: (*a little flustered by this thought*) Oh . . . (*pause*) . . . so that's how Thou knowest . . . I mean, that's how you know?

GOD: (*gently teasing*) So if I know, and you know that I know, why must you keep on trying to tell me?

JANE: (*sighs*) Yes, I see. May I go on now?

GOD: You *may*. I'm not sure that you *can*. But, continue.

JANE: Our loving and gracious heavenly Father . . . (*pauses, confused; starts again*) Our Father which art in heaven . . . (*still not right*) . . . Lord?
(*getting desperate now*)
Please . . . will you teach me how to pray?

GOD: You have just prayed your first prayer!

*　　　*　　　*

We may pray or we may posture, but we will often find prayer puzzling. If we really think about it, that is. I mean, does God always answer prayer? Let's be quite honest: God sometimes answers 'No'. Paul had a problem. We don't know quite what it was, but he calls it a 'thorn in the flesh' and also refers to a 'messenger of Satan' (see 2 Corinthians 12.7–9). Paul three times asked God to take this thing away from him: Each time he said, 'No!' God doesn't always grant our requests. In a way, almost every time someone dies we have an example of prayer that has not been granted.

But doesn't God make a difference if you get a group of people to pray together about something? Doesn't he *have* to grant their request, if they all agree?

Well now, first of all, is this true in experience? Do we find that when two or three people make a prayer request it is *always* granted? No. I can recall scores of examples where God didn't say Yes to the prayer. I remember a group of missionaries who were very concerned about a new mission station being opened in Ethiopia. The Government permission didn't come through. So on the basis of Matthew 18.19 they prayed that the permit would be granted that week. It wasn't. Now here's the verse they used:

'Again I say to you, if two of you agree on earth about anything they ask, it will be done for them by my Father in heaven.'

Or there's John 14.13: 'Whatever you ask in my name, I will do it.'

Now let's look at the theory that we have built around these verses. Our theory is that if two or more people agree together about something they want God to do, or if even one person prays about something he wants God to do and adds the formula 'and this I ask in Jesus' name', then God has to do it. He *has* to. But there's nothing sadder than the sight of a beautiful theory slain by an ugly fact. There's the beautiful theory, but the ugly fact is that God won't be manipulated like that. He says 'No!' even if a thousand of us agree together, and he says 'No!' even when our prayer *is* made in the name of Jesus.

When theory and experience disagree we ought to look at the theory or at the application of the theory to see where there is an error. There must be an error somewhere. And the error is in our understanding of two phrases 'agree together' and 'in the name of Jesus'. Take the second one first. 'In the name of Jesus' doesn't mean a liturgical formula, a little bit of magic.

Jesus once said to his followers: 'Whoever receives this child in my name, receives me.'

Jesus also warned his followers: 'Many will come in my name.'

This phrase has different meanings, but basically it means 'like me', or 'for me' or 'as my representative'. Doing things 'in the name' of Jesus is doing them as he would do them. Asking things 'in the name' of Jesus means asking as he would ask. But how would Jesus do things? How *did* Jesus do things?

First of all, the negative: 'Truly, truly I say to you, the Son can do nothing of his own accord.' (John 5.19)

And secondly, the positive: 'I seek not my own will, but the will of him who sent me.' (John 5.30)

So, 'in my name' means 'as Jesus did things'. And Jesus did things 'in the Father's name', as the Father did them.

Now, agreeing *together*. This explanation, exhortation, came from Donald Barnhouse. It has helped me often. The Greek word that is used here is the word *sumphōneō*. You can just look at the word and guess that it's the word from which we get our English word 'symphony'. Now how do we get

76

symphony? From an orchestra. More precisely, from an orchestra playing together. Now as Donald Barnhouse pointed out, if the double-bass agrees with the pianist that they will play Rachmaninoff, but the score in front of them is Brahms, there won't be any symphony. Maybe they don't like Brahms; perhaps there isn't much for the pianist or too much for the double-bass. But they won't get harmony by agreeing together to play something else. Or maybe Brahms is too difficult for them and they really feel that they would do a better job with Rachmaninoff. They still won't get harmony, they won't produce symphony. They'd get closer to it by staying with the score, even if it is difficult.

You see, in producing a symphony we need an orchestra. But the most important member of the orchestra is never heard. Without him there *can* be no symphony. The conductor. The players have to agree together with the conductor. Then and only then can the orchestra produce a symphony.

That's life. God has the score in front of him. He wrote it. Maybe the part he wrote for me isn't very exciting. Or too exciting. Or too difficult. But it's hopeless for me to go to my friend and say to him: 'Look, I don't like this piece. It's dark. I can't see the purpose of it. I think we need a different score. And he agrees. And we decide that God is just going to have to play our tune. He won't. Far better for us to play the score in front of us as Jesus did. In Jesus' name. To say:

'Lord, I don't understand this passage. It's too hard for me. It seems dark and difficult. Still, not my will, but yours. Help me to play this particular piece, to walk this stretch of life in a way that will please you.'

And when a church in trouble, or a family divided, or friends quarrelling, can pray like that . . . two or three of them . . . God hears and answers and helps them to play the piece, to live the life as they want to . . . as he wants them to.

But praying isn't for publication. That is the last point I want to make in this chapter. If you learn how to discipline your life to make time for prayer: don't publicise the fact. If you do, other Christians will think you're wonderful, but that will be all the reward you get. There *is* a place for public prayer: in the church. Amongst Christians. But although prayer may be public, it's not for publication and it's not for publicity and it's not to be publicised. For if it is, the prayer stops even before it hits the ceiling. Prayer is talking with God, finding out his plans, reading his score, and then asking him to help us to play our little bit in his great symphony.

So then . . . how to pray. Find out what God wants to do in this situation that you're in *now*. Don't tell him what you think he ought to do. Ask him what he wants to do. You may need to wait until he shows you. But when he does show you, don't try to gang up on God . . . pray as Jesus did: 'Father glorify your name. Help me to play this part to your glory.'

They have had their reward

Have you seen Joseph Pinker, the Vicar of Bray
Have you seen his good works in the village all day?
> You couldn't have missed 'im, 'e makes such a show,
> We know Reverend Pinker . . . as Holy Joe!
> Joe 'as 'ad 'is reward in the praises of men
> And God ain't going to give it 'im over again.

Have you see William Braggins, when toiling in prayer
How he's pleading and weeping and tearing his hair?
> You can 'ear 'im all night, famous Bellowing Bill
> 'cos 'e shouts all 'is prayers from the top of a 'ill!
> Bill 'as 'ad 'is reward in the praises of men
> And God ain't going to give it 'im over again.

Have you seen Brother Alfred, as thin as a rake,
How he fasts twice a week for the kingdom's sake?
> Yes, I've seen Alf's long face like a pouring wet week,
> His red nose and 'is eyes with a permanent leak;
> Alf 'as 'ad 'is reward in the praises of men
> And God ain't going to give it 'im over again.

Holy Joe, Brother Alf and that Bellowing Bill
Make the rest of us sinners feel queasy and ill;

Their churches are empty and empty they'll stay:
If *that* is religion we'll go our own way.
They 'ave 'ad their reward in the praises of men
And God ain't going to give it 'em over again.

THINK IT THROUGH

1. Think about the various occasions when we pray:
   when we are alone
   in a prayer meeting
   when the minister leads public prayer.
What are the similarities and what are the differences between these different forms of prayer?
2. Follow the story of Paul's planned visit to Rome. Read:
   Romans 1.8–15
   Romans 15.22–32
   Acts 21.17–36
   Acts 28.11–16.
It has been suggested that God refused the *letter* of Paul's prayer request, but granted the *spirit* of his request. What did Paul ask the Christians at Rome to pray for? What was the spirit of the prayer? Do you agree that God refused the letter but granted the spirit of the prayer?
3. Try to read either chapter 4 in Spurgeon's *Lectures to my Students* or chapter 8 of James Black's *The Mystery of Preaching*. Both passages are about prayer, but particularly about praying in public.

What preparation should be made for praying in public?

What is the advantage of *reading* prayers? What is the disadvantage? What is the advantage of extempore prayer? What is the disadvantage?

CHAPTER 8

Way to Go

I want to know which college I should apply to, which job I ought to take, which fellow I ought to marry. Some time fairly soon I'm going to have to make a decision. How can I be sure that I'm in harmony with what God wants?

Well, the first step is to *want* guidance and to ask God for it.

Actually, even this very first step can prove to be a great help, because when we have to frame a request we need to know what the problem is and what the possible solutions are. I need to get a job, and I've been offered three. I feel that I need some Bible training and someone has suggested Durham. I really like this guy, but I'm not sure that he's a Christian.

Before we go any further, just one comment. In some ways being a Christian becomes easier as you get older. In *some* ways. The older Christian has experience. If you have had to trust God, and you've seen the way in which he works things out, it becomes easier to trust him again. That's how it is with guidance. I have experienced his guidance over and over again, and now I know that I was stupid to worry about guidance. When I wanted to be guided I was guided. One piece of advice I would give to every Christian at the beginning is: don't *worry* about guidance. God *will* guide you. You'll *see* it later, perhaps, but if you *want* God to guide you then he will.

So, first of all, desire guidance, ask for it, expect it. And it will come.

Next, five sources of guidance. They're not in any particular order of importance because God often seems to use them in different combinations to fit the circumstances.

And that brings us to the first source of guidance: *circum-*

stances. Circumstances are like a feather bed: fine, just so long as you're on top. Sometimes circumstances do seem to get on top of us. And there are times when God allows circumstances to get on top of us so that we *have* to do what we are unwilling to do. It was circumstances that drove the missionaries out of Ethiopia in 1937. The Italians invaded the country and ousted the missionaries. It's most unlikely that they would have gone under any other circumstances. God had a job he wanted to do and he couldn't do it while the missionaries were there. So out they went. While they were away, the church grew from about one hundred believers to at least ten thousand. And the church created its own orders for worship and its own organisation. They couldn't have done that with the missionaries there.

Circumstances can include my own particular gifts. If I have no gift for speaking in public then there's not much point in my thinking of being a preacher, and if I can't stand the sight of blood then probably I shouldn't plan on being a nurse. Just a word of warning, or maybe it's really encouragement. Some of the circumstances may need to be ignored. Money, for example. After I'd finished studying physics, I felt that I should go to Spurgeon's College for Bible training. But I had no money. However, I felt quite sure that I was meant to go there and nowhere else. Fortunately the Principal agreed with me that I should go. He, too, felt sure that something would turn up for finances. And it did. Eventually. But the money side of the circumstances had to be ignored. In making the decision, that is. Obviously the money circumstances can't be ignored entirely!

Now there is a second side to this matter of circumstances. If I feel it right to get married, I shan't make much progress if I join a monastery or enter a convent. If I feel called to be a tennis champion then I'd better get where people play tennis. For this aspect of circumstances I offer the word *exposure*. Expose yourself in the areas into which you feel God is leading you. If you feel it is right to go to a university then get brochures from the universities. If you feel an interest in work overseas then write to missionaries and mission societies and go to missionary meetings. If you want Bible training then write to some Bible colleges and visit them. Talk to students.

The second source of guidance is the Holy Spirit. He guides us in two quite distinct ways: through the *inward witness* and through the *outward witness*.

Inwardly we may suddenly come to total certainty about what God wants us to do without having any tangible experience at all. I was a young Christian at the time of the death of King George VI. The following Sunday evening, during the usual service at my church, I felt quite sure that God wanted me to hold a service in a nearby café. I'd been in there quite often, on a Sunday evening, talking with the young folks who always seemed to hang around there. But it's a different matter to hold a service in a café! I went to talk this feeling over with my 'father confessor' as I liked to think of him, the man who led me to Christ. I explained. I expected that he would tell me that this was a very foolish and quite impracticable idea. He didn't. 'You go, I'll be praying for you.'

So I went. First I spoke with the café-owner: Could I hold a service in his café? I expected a good laugh. Instead: 'Sure, if the guys agree.' I turned to the guys. Could we have a service? Again I expected a laugh. Instead, 'Sure, why not?' So we had a service. They only knew one hymn, 'Abide with me', the hymn they always used to sing at the Wembley Cup Final. One of the fellows read from the Bible and I preached.

I knew I ought to go and do it. I went and I did it.

But there is also the outward witness of the Spirit, through the Bible. Now this one is full of pitfalls. Opening your Bible at random and just stabbing the page may lead to guidance, or it may not. There are too many funny stories told about guidance obtained in this way for it to *be* funny. But God guides from the Bible in other ways, too. He *may* give you one verse, when you throw open your Bible at random. But he may throw just one verse at you, clunk, clunk, clunk, just like that, from all directions. When the Bible comes at you like that, then is the time to pay attention.

Again, the Bible can be used by the Spirit to guide us through its teaching. If you want to do something that is against the teaching of the Bible, then you don't need any more guidance than you've got. If you're tied up with a fellow who isn't a Christian and you want guidance as to whether you should marry him or not, well the Spirit will give you guidance right from the Bible. There it is, 2 Corinthians 6:14: 'Don't be teamed with those who do not love the Lord, for what do the people of God have in common with the people of sin? How can light live with darkness? And what harmony can there be between Christ and the devil? How can a Christian be a partner with one who doesn't believe?'

God guides us through the Spirit and the Bible which was inspired by the Spirit. For a good many decisions you don't need any guidance beyond what you've got.

So, we are guided by circumstances. We are guided by the inward witness of the Spirit (we just *know*, inside) and by the outward witness of the Spirit, through the Bible. Fourthly we are guided through prayer.

We've already seen that prayer is dialogue, not monologue. I talk with God and he talks with me. So if I need guidance I can talk to him about it and I can expect that he will reply . . . if I give him the chance to do it. No, I can't say that I have ever heard God speaking to me as an audible voice. But often there is just no other way for us to explain what has happened when we have prayed for guidance than: 'God said to me . . .', 'God told me . . .'

I don't *know*, but I suspect that when the prophets of the Old Testament wrote, 'The Word of the Lord came to me, saying . . .', or 'Then the Lord said to me . . .' that's what they meant. They didn't hear a voice. But they heard God speaking. His voice isn't heard with ears made out of cartilage and the rest of it, but it's heard in the spirit.

Lastly: get advice. What are older Christians for if not to share their experiences with us? Maybe *we* haven't passed this way before but *they* probably have. Experience counts. And unfortunately the only way to get experience is to get experience. You don't find it in books. Older Christians have got it. So be ready to make use of their experience. Ask people for advice when they've been through some similar experience to yours. But a word of warning: beware of the temptation to tip the scales in the direction you want them to go, by choosing someone whose advice you can be pretty sure will coincide with your plans. And again, grey hair and grey matter don't necessarily belong together. So be careful who you ask for advice. Ask someone who commands respect.

WHAT THE BIBLE SAYS

Acts 16.6–10
Next Paul and Silas travelled through Phrygia and Galatia, because the Holy Spirit had told them not to go into the Turkish province of Ausia at that time. Then, going along the borders of Mysia they headed north for the province of Bithynia, but again the Spirit of Jesus said no. So instead they went on through Mysia province to the city of Troas. That night Paul had a vision. In his dream he saw a man over in Macedonia, Greece, pleading with him, 'Come over here and help us.' Well, that settled it. We would go to Macedonia, for we could only conclude that God was sending us to preach the Good News there.

Isaiah 30.21
If you leave God's paths and go astray, you will hear a Voice behind you say, 'No, this is the way; walk here.'

WHICH WAY TO GO?

When we read about Paul's travels we are astonished at the way in which his guidance is described:
    'The Holy Spirit had told them . . .'
    'The Spirit of Jesus said no . . .'
    'Paul had a vision . . . that settled it . . .'
If we put those experiences along with the verse in Isaiah we can see that there is a sense in which normally God leaves

us alone. He doesn't keep saying: turn left here, watch those pedestrians, you only just missed that parked car ... like some omnipresent driving instructor. Instead God sets us on our way and tunes back in again just as soon as we begin to go off course: 'If you leave God's paths ...' He trusts us to keep on going once we have found his way. But he's there if we need him. Unfortunately we don't always want his guidance. We may *know* what he wants us to do, but we have no intention of doing it. If we are used to pious self-deception we may go to the minister for advice, or we may 'pray about it' or stick a pin into the Bible ...

*   *   *

Marian is dressed in jeans and has a pack of some kind over her shoulder. In one hand she carries a short stick. In the other hand she holds a rolled-up map. She walks on, as George walks on from the opposite direction. George stands and watches her. She sets her pack down, unrolls the map. Squints at it very carefully. Turns it this way and that. Sighs. Then throws down her stick, looks at it carefully, shakes her head. Picks the stick up again, throws it down again. And again sighs, shakes her head and retrieves the stick. The process is repeated a third time. George comes closer and closer to her, obviously intrigued by what she is doing. When he speaks she jumps:

GEORGE: (*curious*) Excuse me ... sorry if I scared you ... but could you explain what you are doing?
MARIAN: What I'm doing?
GEORGE: Yes ... what's all this business with the stick?
MARIAN: Oh, the stick? Yes, that's my guide.
GEORGE: The stick is your guide?
MARIAN: Oh yes ... the stick is my guide. Every time I come to a crossroads I throw down my stick and if it points straight ahead I go straight ahead and if it points to the left fork I turn left and if it ...
GEORGE: Yes, I get it, if it points to the right you turn to the right. But why do you keep throwing it down like that?

85

MARIAN: Well, it keeps on pointing to the right, and I want to go left.

GEORGE: Ummmm . . . Why do you want to go left, by the way?

MARIAN: Well, it might be my political convictions . . . but it's not. Oh no. It's my map.

GEORGE: So you do have a map?

MARIAN: Oh yes, a very good map. A little old. A little torn perhaps, but a very good map. *Beeaauutifully* printed. In eight colours.

GEORGE: May I see? . . . ummm . . . which way is north?

MARIAN: North? I don't really know. Isn't it marked? I suppose it really ought to be marked somehow. But as I don't know this district very well, I don't know *your* north, and I'm not clever enough to use a compass, so I just use the map, you see.

GEORGE: I can see how often you must get lost . . . Now, where are we on this wonderful map?

MARIAN: Well . . . I thought probably somewhere about here. (*points to the map*) Up in this left hand corner, perhaps. There don't seem to be many houses marked on the map and there aren't many houses around here, so this *could* be the spot, don't you think?

GEORGE: What I think would probably shock you. Look, why did you want to turn left?

MARIAN: Did I want to turn left? Oh yes, perhaps I did. Well you see, according to this beautiful map, if I turn left I should get on to this marvellous road that's marked here with a double line. And I thought that with such a *big* road I'd be quite sure to get a lift. Perhaps its a motorway.

GEORGE: If it *is* a motorway pedestrians aren't allowed on it. Here, let me look at the map . . . (*studies it for a moment, twisting it around a bit*) Here, wait a minute . . . (*whistles*) You don't want to get on to that double line you know . . . that just happens to be the main runway of the airport!

MARIAN: Oh, but it can't be . . . there isn't any airport here.

GEORGE: No, there isn't. But this map isn't a map of this area at all. It's a map of Paris. And that is Orly Airport. Or it *was*.

MARIAN: What do you mean it was Orly Airport?

GEORGE: The date on this map is 1926. It's just a little bit out of date!

MARIAN: (*admiring*) Oh, aren't you clever ... (*thinks a moment*) Well, it's just as well that I've got my stick to guide me isn't it? Here, let me try once more ... (*throws the stick down again, peers at it, gives a little gasp of delight*)

You see, it works. It's all right. It points left. (*thinks*) Something wrong there ... how can it be all right when it points left? Never mind ... on we go ... guided, always wonderfully guided ... (*she burbles off*)

GEORGE: But *how* she's guided and *where* she'll end up is anyone's guess. I suppose I'd better follow her to see that she doesn't get guided into the duck pond ... (*George follows her out*)

*　　*　　*

The very idea of guidance assumes that God has a plan that is so detailed that it even takes my little life into it. The idea of guidance also assumes that God is willing to show me my part. But when I try to manipulate God, to get him to change his plan for my life, when I try to ignore the Voice that says 'No, *this* is the way', I'm simply showing that I don't trust God. But believe me, His plan for your life is good, it is perfect and it is acceptable (Romans 12.2): 'Do not be conformed to this world but be transformed, by the renewal of your mind, that you may prove what is the will of God, what is good and acceptable and perfect.' (RSV)

Don't be afraid of God's will. It's good. Before you were a Christian you didn't trust God. Now your mind has been 'renewed', changed. So now you *can* trust God. Trust him when he says: 'My will for your life is good. My will for your life can't be improved on: it's perfect.' Your part is to say simply:

'All right ... then I can accept it.'

One final thought. On guidance. Some Christians have got so mixed up in their ideas about God that they really do think that if they would *like* to do something then it has to be wrong. If they want to get married then they should probably stay single. If they'd like to go to college then probably they should become odd-job gardeners.

God wants us to be happy! He wants us to rejoice. Some of us are determined to be miserable. No! It *is* hard to be a Christian, but it's a marvellous life. A life to be enjoyed. Of course there will be problems, but God really doesn't want us to give up laughter for the duration. Thank God for those who make us laugh. No, don't become one of those fatuous people who go round with a determined bright smile on the face whatever may be their state of mind. But life is good. God is good. And he gives his children good gifts, good lives. Don't refuse his guidance just because you like the look of it!

And lastly a few pithy, pointed principles:

You won't get guidance until you need it.

You may not need more guidance than you've got.

It's when you take the *wrong* path that you hear God's voice.

Move when you *must*, not when you *may*.

When in doubt – wait.

God's will is good, acceptable and *perfect*.

THINK IT THROUGH

1. Share your experiences of God's guidance. Discuss these experiences. Did you recognise God's guidance *before* the change, *during* the change or *afterwards*? How did the guidance come? Did you just *know* . . . or was it from the Bible . . . or through someone's advice . . . or maybe a vision?

2. Spurgeon was definitely guided *not* to go to university. He was to preach one Sunday at Chesterton and he says:

'I walked slowly, in a meditative frame of mind, over Midsummer Common to the little wooden bridge which leads to Chesterton, and in the midst of the Common I was startled by what seemed a loud voice, but which may have been a singular illusion. Whichever it was, the impression was vivid to an intense degree; I seemed very distinctly to hear the words, "Seekest thou great things for thyself? Seek them not!" This led me to look at my position from another point of view and to challenge my motives and intentions.'

Spurgeon was, apparently, well qualified to enter Stepney College, now Regents Park College. But he never did. Read the remarkable account of his experiences while seeking admission there, in his autobiography.

What is the value of university training? What is the danger of it? Why was it denied to Spurgeon? How do you explain the voice that he heard? Find similar examples in the Bible.

3. How would you advise a young Christian to go about the business of getting guidance for his first job?

CHAPTER 9

Tell It Like It Is

This chapter is about witnessing. But I don't really like that label because it has an institutional look about it. There are manuals of witnessing. There are principles of witnessing. There are theories about it. Witnessing shades off into evangelism, and there are systems of evangelism, methods of evangelism and you can buy complete do-it-yourself evangelism packs.

What I really want to talk about in this chapter is simply telling people about Jesus. About God. About what God has done for me. And I'm spoiled. Let me explain. I've lived most of my Christian life in Africa. And there, when people became Christians they *knew* that something wonderful had happened to them. Two things really stuck in their minds: they were no longer afraid of evil spirits and they were no longer afraid to die. They could make their farms in the lowland areas which they had thought to be the special property of the devils. They could brush aside the demands of the *shamans*, the 'witch-doctors'.

And by the way, don't let some trendy teacher tell you that the African was better off without the missionary, that his own religion suited him, that the witch-doctor was a good influence. Sorry ... that's just well-meaning bunk. I am often asked: didn't you missionaries interfere with the culture of the people? And I reply, without any apology, We certainly did. For example. In Aden, one standard treatment for dysentery was to place a red-hot coal on the baby's stomach to drive out the devil causing the dysentery. We did our best to stop that practice. In Ethiopia, the same trouble was fixed by cutting out the baby's eye-teeth. And they stopped the uvula from growing down the baby's throat and choking him to death, by cutting it out: with an old razor blade if the baby was fortunate; with a dirty piece of flint otherwise. And we tried to stop that practice. In Nigeria, twins were bad news and both babies were disposed of. We tried to stop that. And that's the kind of interfering ignoramuses we were. No, the people weren't better off without the missionary. We made our mistakes, but we did a lot of good. As one Christian said to me, pointing to the flourishing farms around him:

'When you missionaries brought us the gospel, you brought so much more than the gospel.'

They knew how good the gospel was. So they told people about Jesus. What he'd done for them. They didn't go to a Bible college to be educated in it, and they didn't buy a *Teach Yourself to Evangelise* handbook. They gossiped the gospel and the church grew mightily ... unlike the church over here ...

THE ORANGE-PICKERS' FELLOWSHIP

The idea for this skit comes from a tract. A little more preparation than usual is needed if you want to put this skit on. In particular you need an orange tree. Any leafy bough will do: tie the oranges on carefully, with cotton. They need to be secure enough so that they won't fall off during the skit, but at least two should be loose enough to come off when 'picked' without the orange picking pulling the whole tree down.

George and Henry walk in from opposite sides. There is a 'congregation' of a dozen or so. Dr William Silvermouth is the preacher. He has a box of some kind to stand on.

GEORGE: Well, here I am! I bet you're surprised to see me here!
HENRY: Surprised! I should say so ... you always said that you didn't really agree with picking oranges ... You *have* come to help with the orange harvest haven't you?
GEORGE: Yes ... I started thinking about what that lecturer said about the need for us all to help with the oranges;

you know, 'The harvest is plenteous but the labourers are few', so I thought I should help. When do we start?

HENRY: Well, you've really chosen a good day to come. This is Orange Day. Today we pick oranges.

GEORGE: What about tomorrow? Can't we pick oranges tomorrow, too?

HENRY: (*disconcerted, but swiftly rallies*) Well ... you *can* pick oranges any day. One should always be prepared to pick oranges. But we like to set aside one day of the week especially for the picking of oranges. (*confidently*) It's so good to be able to turn aside from other tasks and give one whole day to this vital task.

GEORGE: Well, okay ... let's start picking.

HENRY: Now wait a minute. You can't just start picking oranges. You don't know anything about the subject. Let me tell you, there are people who have devoted a lifetime to the study of orange-picking techniques, the development of new programmes, a consideration of the modular approach and there's a new book just published on the influence of transcendental meditation on orange-picking.

GEORGE: Eh? All I know is, you put out your hand, grab hold of an orange and ...

HENRY: (*shocked*) Grab hold of an orange! You can't just go around grabbing hold of oranges. There are proper techniques to be mastered. You've got a *lot* to learn. But never mind ... here's the Area Superintendent of the Orange Pickers' Fellowship. He's our teacher ... He's an inspiration to everybody, especially to the young people ... (*Silvermouth enters. He carries a large folder, prominently labelled 'Orange-pickers' Manual'. He climbs on to the box. Everyone gathers round*)

SILVERMOUTH: My very dear friends, it rejoices my heart to see you all gathered here in expectancy on this another glorious Orange Day. Let us sing in opening just the first verse of the Orange-pickers' theme song, 'Will the orange-blossom flourish?'

(*all sing, to the tune 'What a friend we have in Jesus'*)

> Will the orange blossom flourish?
> Will the fruit be gathered in?

Oranges can feed and nourish
Let us now the task begin.

Vitamins are sorely needed
Oranges can save the ill;
Souls for oranges have pleaded
And they're pleading for them still.

GEORGE: (*getting impatient*) Okay, Okay . . . now do we start picking oranges?

HENRY: Patience, patience. First of all the Area Superintendent expounds a chapter or so from the new translation of the Orange-Pickers' Manual. He's been to Manual school, you know: four years of concentrated study.

GEORGE: (*not impressed*) Studying *what*?

HENRY: How to pick oranges, stupid. They study the Manual in the original languages. They have the biggest Manual college in the country. William of Orange is their patron saint. And they're really fundamental, too. No compromise. Coca-Cola is banned: everyone drinks orange juice.

SILVERMOUTH: (*orates*) Beloved, I feel that it is high time that we exerted ourselves. I do realise my debt to you all. Without your continuing faithful support I could do nothing, absolutely nothing. Together . . . together nothing is impossible. Not even picking these oranges is beyond us.

HENRY: Isn't he marvellous? A real inspiration. I think he's going to make an appeal, too. He often does.

SILVERMOUTH: Now I want to challenge you . . . to stand with me, by faith, for the picking of an orange. How many of you are ready for this great step of faith? For this test of obedience? If we stand together, nothing doubting, convinced that the job *can* be done, then it *shall* be done. Let us stand together . . .

(*all gather round him as he steps down from the box and approaches the orange tree. Make sure that the audience can still clearly see him.*

He hesitates, inspects the oranges carefully, stretches out a hand, flexes his fingers. There are admiring looks

93

*from the crowd, indrawn breath, ooohs and aaahs. He
hovers indecisively between two oranges. His audience
jostle each other in their excitement. George stands
watching, his mouth wide open. Finally, with a flourish,
and a neat turn of the wrist Silvermouth manages to pick
an orange. He holds it up. Spontaneous applause. Shouts
of 'Amen' ...)*

HENRY: See he did it, he did it! Did you see that? Fantastic! I
guess you can see now what an art there is to this thing?

GEORGE: (*unimpressed*) Okay ... now do we get to pick
oranges? (*looks around as the crowd begins to drift away*)
Where are they going?

HENRY: Home, of course. The Orange-Day service is over.
See you next week.

(*he follows the rest out. George is left alone*)

GEORGE: (*looks at the tree, still loaded with oranges*) It looks
simple enough to me ... (*stretches out a hand, touches an
orange, hesitates, then picks it*) It *is* easy. (*looks at the rest
of the fruit*) But I suppose that Area Superintendent must
know more about it than I do ... there must be a mystery
somewhere. Maybe I should go to Manual college . (*walks
off. Group sings from outside*

> Vitamins are sorely needed
> Oranges can save the ill;
> Souls for oranges have pleaded
> And they're pleading for them still.)

HAT THE BIBLE TEACHES

Mark 3.13–19

Jesus went up into the hills and summoned certain ones he
chose, inviting them to come and join him there; and they
did. Then he selected twelve of them to be his regular com-
panions and to go out to preach, and to cast out demons.
These are the names of the twelve he chose:

Simon (he renamed him 'Peter'),

James and John (the sons of Zebedee, but Jesus called
them 'Sons of Thunder',

Andrew, Philip,
Bartholomew, Matthew,
Thomas,
James (the son of Alphaeus),
Thaddaeus,
Simon (a member of a political party advocating violent overthrow of the Roman government),
Judas Iscariot (who later betrayed him).

Matthew 28.18–20
Jesus told his disciples:
'I have been given all authority in heaven and earth.
Therefore go and make disciples in all the nations, baptising them into the name of the Father and of the Son and of the Holy Spirit,
and then teach these new disciples to obey all the commands I have given you;
and be sure of this – that I am with you always,
even to the end of the world.'

Acts 1.8 (RSV)
You shall be my witnesses.

Acts 4.1–13 (RSV)
And as the disciples were speaking to the people, the priests and the captain of the temple and the Sadducees came upon them, annoyed because they were teaching the people and proclaiming in Jesus the resurrection from the dead. And they arrested them and put them in custody until the morrow, for it was already evening. But many of those who heard the word believed; and the number of the men came to about five thousand.

On the morrow their rulers and elders and scribes were gathered together in Jerusalem, with Annas the high priest and Caiaphas and John and Alexander, and all who were of the high priestly family. And when they had set them in the midst, they inquired, 'By what power or by what name did you do this?'

Then Peter, filled with the Holy Spirit, said to them,

'Rulers of the people, and elders, if we are being examined today concerning a good deed done to a cripple, by what means this man has been healed, be it known to you all, and to all the people of Israel, that by the name of Jesus Christ of Nazareth, whom you crucified, whom God raised from the dead, by him this man is standing before you well. This is the stone which was rejected by you builders, but which has become the head of the corner. And there is salvation in no one else, for there is no other name under heaven, given among men, by which we must be saved.'

Now when they saw the boldness of Peter and John, and perceived that they were uneducated, common men, they wondered; and they recognised that they had been with Jesus.

Acts 4.20 (RSV)
... we cannot but speak of what we have seen and heard.

BUT HOW IS IT?

It's all very well to say 'Tell it like it is', but our biggest problem, where 'witnessing' is concerned, is to know just how it *is*. What *has* God done for you?

Well, go on ... try writing down, without using a lot of theological words, what God has done for you. You can't really use theological words in sharing the Good News because people don't understand the language. So, quite simply, what has God done for you?

The Christians in Ethiopia, in the far south at least, would have replied:

I have lost my fear of evil spirits.

I have lost my fear of death.

Now that would be good enough news to make a real impression.

So what might *we* say? Here are a few suggestions:

I now have a purpose in life.

I'm no longer afraid of the future.

I don't have any hang-ups about my past.

96

I've got friends.
When things go wrong I can pray about them.
God helps me with my bad temper.
I know that history is HIS STORY. Events aren't haphazard.
I'm finding that I really can love other people.
I'm thankful now for even the little things of life;
  I know that millions of others haven't got them.
  I know that God trusts me with them.
  I know that things aren't to be used selfishly.
I find the world so much more *real*: sunset and moonrise,
  storm and calm, wind and rain, packed houses and
  quiet villages and noisy cities all remind me that
  God loves me . . . and loves us all.

Now if this is the kind of 'testimony' that we should be able to give, we'd better be careful to distinguish it from *preaching*. We're acting as witnesses, telling people 'of what we have seen and heard' and what it has meant to us. These new experiences of ours we ascribe to Jesus. And when people ask to know more about this new quality of life that we have, then we can *preach*. Tell them who Jesus is, how he died for them, how he rose again and how he commands all people, everywhere to repent.

But let's go back a bit. I mentioned the likelihood of people asking 'to know more about this new quality of life we have'.

They won't ask if we haven't got it.

They'll know we haven't got it . . . or if we have got it . . . only if they know us.

So I think I want to divide the witness of the church into two categories.

Christians live strikingly different lives: they love one another, they are not afraid of the future, they can face trouble, illness, even death, with courage, they are helpful, they have unusually happy homes, and they show these lives to their neighbours who are impressed with the simple fact of a changed life. And then someone gets the opportunity to tell the neighbours about Jesus. About his life and death. So that when the minister from the local church decides to visit

-D

a few homes in your street, the people he visits will respond at once:

'Oh yes, I know ... like that Mrs Goodson in number thirty-five. I've often wondered what it was that made her so different. When I was ill, you know, she was round here in a flash, made the beds and helped Jim with the dinner and away off home again as though it was the most natural thing in the world. No fuss ... Yes, I'd like to know a bit more ...'

Now of course, the snag with all this is obvious. What if Mrs Goodson hasn't got it? The new kind of life, I mean? What if she does go to the church, but she's cantankerous, quarrelsome, fights with her husband, argues with the milkman, and nourishes a generous crop of dandelions whose seeds regularly infest the gardens of all her neighbours for a hundred yards around?

All the Explosive Evangelistic Expertise in the world won't make an impact on the neighbours. They can already see that It Doesn't Work. And after all, that's the only test of Christianity. We can't *prove* that Jesus was crucified for our sins and we can't *prove* that he rose from the grave and now lives in my life. Show me! That's the reaction of the neighbours. You show me someone whose life really *is* different and then I'll be ready to listen to your preachers.

And this is where I have very little faith in most of our evangelistic techniques. They're not bad in themselves. But.

They dodge a fundamental principle of Christian living and church growth. *Discipling must begin where it broke off.*

Let me explain. In the book of Judges we have the 'sin cycle' set out for us. The Jews were given a certain kind of life to live. It was a life of faith and that also means a life of obedience. They didn't live it. So God turned them over to some foreign power and they suffered. Until eventually someone woke up and said:

'Men, this is ridiculous. We're God's people. We ought not to live as slaves of these foreigners. God has let this happen to us because we left him out of our lives.'

And the response of the people was:

'Well, what do we do now?'

98

'Repent!'

So the people repented. They turned away from whatever sin it was that was ruining their lives and started praying again. Praying and obeying. And then God heard their prayers and answered their prayers and sent some leader to set them free. Read Judges for yourself. The cycle goes round and round and always in the same order: obedience, rebellion, punishment, repentance, deliverance. In Judges chapter 3 we have Othniel as the leader who saves the repentant people from the Mesopotamians. From verse 15 of that chapter it's the Moabites who enslave them and Ehud who delivers them. In chapter 4, Deborah and Barak deal with the Canaanites. And so the wheel goes round and round.

There's a similar sort of cycle for Christians. It's the cycle of evangelism. It begins with preaching the Good News. Then people believe it. Those who believe are taught what God expects of them and they obey him. Because they obey him their lives demonstrate the new life that Christ gives so that again the gospel is preached through them, people are saved and then *they* are taught and *they* obey God. So God blesses *them* and *their* lives demonstrate the new life that Christ has given *them* and so the gospel is preached and through *them* more people become Christians and . . .

Now that's not just a repetitive cycle. The picture is not of a circle, but of a spiral, getting larger each time around. Obviously it will. Each fresh group of Christians will be reaching out to fresh neighbours. Western Avenue, then Park Street and The Close and Manor Road and . . .

But here's the point. If the spiral is broken anywhere, then the spiral will only take off again if it is begun at the point where it was broken off. You can't jump a spoke in the wheel.

We'll suppose that the minister of the church has stopped teaching the Christians about the kind of life they ought to be living. He may preach evangelism all the time. He may preach socially relevant sermons (as if the Christian life is irrelevant!)' But he doesn't teach the people: 'don't lie, families stick together, pray at all times, pay your debts, thank

God over the washing up, visit the sick . . .' and so on. Then the quality of Christian life is impoverished. People can't find the way. Neighbours don't see that *this* is the way it is when you're a Christian and isn't it marvellous? Instead they see . . . So *this* is the way of life when you're a Christian . . . isn't it ridiculous? And when the minister cheerfully knocks on the door a few minutes later it's not surprising that even the latest evangelistic system has no attraction.

And it will be a waste of time for the church to organise 'outreach'. The breakdown has occurred at the point of *teaching*. So the people must be *taught* again before the spiral can be mended.

Or maybe the pastor *is* faithfully teaching, but the people aren't obeying. Well then it's the responsibility now, not of the minister, but of the people, to repent. To live up to what they already know. And once again, it will be a waste of time for evangelistic efforts to be organised by the minister. The spiral must be taken up just where it was broken off, at the point of obedience.

You'll have noticed that I'm being almost absurdly prosaic in my description of Christian living. Talking about washing up, and weeding the garden and fighting with the milkman and making the beds for the neighbour who is ill. But I'm not merely trying to be trendy. *That* kind of behaviour will be inevitable if Christianity really does mean 'Christ in you'. Jesus said that he came to us not to be served, but to serve others. And when he comes to us he makes us, too, servants of others. But often we find this very inconvenient. Other people take advantage of us. (As they took advantage of Jesus. He went with his followers for a very brief holiday and the crowds followed him and demanded that he should help them. And Jesus looked at the crowds, and instead of saying, as I might well have done: 'Oh for goodness sake, do go away! I'm on holiday. Can't a man have even *one* day off?' he 'had compassion on them, because they were like sheep without a shepherd'. I think that's marvellous.)

So instead of a certain *quality of life*, which proves to be rather difficult to maintain, we satisfy ourselves with *an orthodox belief.* We have our list of beliefs: in the inspiration of the Bible, the virgin birth, the empty tomb, the coming of Christ and so on. And we hold on to them and assume that as a consequence we must be good Christians.

Now Christian belief *is* important. I believe in all those matters I've just listed. But belief in those matters isn't an end. It's a beginning. It ought to be the beginning of a new way of life. Not merely a new pattern of church-going, but a total new life-style, for which there is no substitute if the church-growth spiral is to go on. Look, for example, at the qualifications Paul passed on to Timothy for a man who felt called to be a pastor:

'A pastor must be a *good* man, whose *life* cannot be spoken against. He must have only one wife, and he must be *hard working* and *thoughtful, orderly* and full of *good deeds*. He must enjoy having *guests in his home* and he must be a good Bible teacher. He must *not be a drinker* or *quarrelsome*, but he must be *gentle and kind*. (1 Timothy 3.2–3)

So, by all means, tell it like it is. But how is it? All theory and no practice? All theology and no Christ-life? One of the most extraordinary sides of church life is the Christian with the saddest face imaginable who talks about 'the joy of the Lord'. It's the weirdest kind of confusion.

I'm glad I'm a Christian

(to be recited in as sad and lugubrious a tone as possible)

Since I first became a Christian I've been happy as can be,
Every day is filled with joy, I'm one great smile as you can see;
Every problem solved for good, and every burden whisked away,
Each day better than the last, and that is why you'll hear me say:
    'I'm a Christian, I'm a Christian, and you'll never find me sad,
    I'm a joyful, happy Christian and I'm glad, glad, glad.'

Full of joy I'm up at six and with my Bible in my hand
I begin each blessed day, this way of life is simply grand.
Half an hour of blessed prayer and half an hour of blessed
song
guarantee a blessed life, a life where nothing can go wrong:
    'I'm a Christian, I'm a Christian and you'll never find
      me sad;
    I'm a joyful happy Christian and I'm glad, glad, glad.'

There are sinners in the street, with faces long and sad and
drear,
And I often go to talk with them and take them words of
cheer,
For they need God's free forgiveness and they need his healing grace
And they need my smiling presence and they need my
cheery face.
    'I'm a Christian, I'm a Christian and you'll never find
      me sad,
    I'm a cheerful, happy Christian and I'm glad, glad,
      glad.'

When I think of all the joy I have, the happiness within,
Just one thing has me worried, although worry *is* a sin:
Though I've tried to spread the light and bring good cheer to
one and all
I have never made a convert and I hear my neighbours call:
    ' 'E's a Christian, 'E's a Christian, and 'is face is long
      and sad;
    Well, we're glad that we ain't Christians, yes we're
      glad, glad, glad.'

Mark you, I don't expect a Christian to develop the Great
Executive Grin. I've seen some preachers who have obviously been to charm school somewhere, and fix a fatuous
grin on their faces as they enter the pulpit but take it off
again when they are safely home. But surely Jesus *did* give
us such a marvellous new life that we *should* be glad? Surely
if we are to rejoice there should be *some* evidence of it on
our faces?

102

The early Christians didn't seem to need Bible college to teach them to share with their neighbours the new life they had received from Christ. Certainly many of the Christians I knew in Ethiopia were illiterate, unlearned (like Peter and John!) ordinary people. But their lives spoke for Jesus.

It's our lives that tell it like it is. Not our lips.

TALK IT OVER

1. What changes has Christ made to your life?
   Try to write down the changes in the order of importance that *your neighbours or friends* might give to them.
2. What system of evangelism does your church use?
   The Sunday evening service?
   House-to-house visiting?
   Through a witness team?
   Guest services?
   Talk to some of those involved in these kinds of witnessing. What do they suggest is the most usual reason for people being 'turned off' Christianity?
3. Do you talk to people about Jesus?
   Why? Or why not?
4. Which is the more important in evangelism: personal witnessing or preaching?

CHAPTER 10

A Cry for Help

A friend of mine used to work for one of the really big companies: several thousand workers and he was just one of the crowd. Then, quite unexpectedly, he got a rise in his salary:

'But I'd got nobody to say thank you to!'

He was really grateful for the rise. It would make quite a bit of difference to him. But who had given it to him? Not the foreman, or even the shop manager. Someone much further up the line. And Charles was grateful, but with no one to thank.

That's frustrating enough. But I wonder what people do when they have problems, and no one to take them to?

CARE OF THE POST OFFICE

George and Harry work in the post office. They are sorting the morning mail before taking it out on their 'walks'. They are a rough and ready pair, although George is inclined to be a little bit sentimental.

The idea for this skit came from Carol Strong, who was with her father and mother, missionaries, in Africa. I don't remember quite how her script developed, but I was very struck with the way she brought God into a place where you don't expect to find him: the post office. Thanks, Carol.

GEORGE: Not too bad this morning; should be finished by eight with this lot. Cor ... what writing! He must have addressed this one in 'is bath!

HARRY: Just as well it *is* an easy load: it's pouring down outside. Hello ... look at this one ... (*louder*) ... Here, George, what would you do with this one?

GEORGE: Let's have a look, then. Cor! Stone the crows! Well, you can't deliver that one this morning ... (*reads*) To God, Heaven, care of the Post Office. Here chuck it in the Dead Letter box with the rest of them ... or else ... tell you what, do like we do at Christmas, with the Santa Claus letters: send it to ... where is it ... Copenhagen?

HARRY: No, hold on a minute, George. The envelope isn't stuck down, see. And it's a kid's writing ... wonder what 'e says?

GEORGE: Funny sort of thing, that, a kid writing to God, care of the Post Office. As if we'd know how to find God. You're right though, it isn't stuck down. Let's have a look at the letter ... (*he pulls the letter out of the envelope*) You read it, Harry.

HARRY: (*reading*) Dear God, I don't really know how to get this letter to you, but our postman will know; he knows everything and he gave me a sweet once, and he works at the post office and he's kind and ...

GEORGE: (*interrupts*) Here, who's it from? Any address on the letter? Cor! It's from that boy down in Walpole Street ... number forty-six. That's *my* walk. (*a bit subdued*) Didn't know he thought I was ... kind.

HARRY: (*reads on*) Dear God, please can you help my Dad because they've made him ... what's this ... (*spells it out*) r-e-d-d-u-d-i-n-g ... Redduding? What's the kid mean?

GEORGE: Let's have a look ... redduding ...? Got it! *Redundant*, that's what he means, redundant. He's quite right: his Dad's been out of work for three months now. *Redundant*.

HARRY: Please can you help my Dad because they've made him redundant and when he's home all the time and can't go to work but stays home all day he gets cross and Mum gets cross too, so please can you help my Dad, Love from Richard.

GEORGE: That's right, Richard, that's 'is name. (*pause*) Well, what do we do with the letter? You can't send that kind of letter to Santa Claus ... I mean, it's not in his department is it? He can't help. Blest if I know what to do with it ... (*picks up the letter and reads it again*) 'Dear God, they've made my father redundant . . .' lots of other folks' Dads, too, mate. And they all get cross when there's nothing to do. But what's the use of telling God about it?

HARRY: Well, *he* thinks it's some use telling God about it, otherwise why write a letter, *and* post it first class mail?

GEORGE: Funny, that . . . it's the kind of stuff they used to teach us when we were in Sunday school.

HARRY: (*really taken with the idea of George in Sunday school*) I never knew you went to Sunday school, George. Can't imagine you with a Bible and hymn book, somehow.

GEORGE: (*musing aloud*) Oh yes . . . till I was fourteen . . . grew out of it then. Didn't seem to do anything for you, somehow. But . . . I dunno. That letter sort of gets me. What *do* we do with it?

HARRY: (*passes the buck*) I don't know what *you're* going to do with it. I'm off. Drop it in with the Dead Letters, like I said. Or . . . tell you what (*passes the buck again*) let the Inspector have it. That's what he's paid for . . . Cheerio!

GEORGE: (*folds the letter up, puts it back in the envelope*) Dear God . . . please can you help my Dad . . . (*pauses, then reluctantly drops it into the Dead Letter box*) How can you send a letter to God? (*picks up his bag and walks out*)

WHAT THE BIBLE SAYS

Psalm 139.17–18
How precious it is, Lord, to realise that you are thinking about me constantly! I can't even count how many times a day your thoughts turn towards me. And when I waken in the morning, you are still thinking of me!

Matthew 9.35–36
Wherever Jesus went he healed people of every sort of illness. And what pity he felt for the crowds that came, be-

cause their problems were so great, and they didn't know what to do, or where to go for help.

BUT WHAT CAN GOD DO ABOUT IT?

There are really only two kinds of problem: the problem you can cope with and the problem you can't cope with. If you're hungry but you have a bar of chocolate in your pocket, you have a problem which you can solve: take the chocolate out of your pocket and eat it. But if your car breaks down on a back road, in the middle of the night when you're on the way to hospital with your wife who is expecting a baby, you have a problem which you probably can't solve by yourself.

Insoluble problems. Even children have them. Children who stay up too late and simply don't know what to do with their tiredness. I watched one little girl literally bang her head on the floor in sheer frustration when she had that problem. Grown-ups don't do that; instead they take it out on the children or the neighbours or their wives.

Of course, the state does its best to help us with our problems. But in fact, the state often can't touch the real problems, in spite of the welfare programmes available. When Richard's Dad lost his job, he didn't want unemployment benefit: he wanted work. He may even have received the 'golden handshake' when he left his work, but the money wasn't the issue. Without work life seemed pointless. So he took it out on the family.

Richard's problem wasn't that his Dad was out of work. What he wanted was to get his Dad back: the real, contented Dad that Richard was used to, the Dad Richard loved. But the Welfare State can't arrange that. Man has to learn to live by bread alone.

And when no one else could help, Richard turned to God. Like a sheep without a shepherd he reached out to the Good Shepherd he had somehow heard about. The time for reaching out to God comes, eventually, to all of us. Eventually we

meet a situation we can't cope with. And then, hopefully, we
cry out: 'God!?' But he doesn't seem to be there . . .

Bethlehem and Birmingham

I've heard of Bethlehem before:
they shelled it in the six-day war,
but Birmingham suits me just fine
with telly and a glass of wine
and radio with 'What's my line?'
You keep your ways and I'll keep mine.

I've heard of Bethlehem before
and Joseph, knocking on the door;
The gaffer said 'e'd got no bed –
if only Joe 'ad used 'is head
and given 'im a quid instead
of all the other things 'e said,
There'd be a room, and meat and bread.

I've heard of Bethlehem before,
I've heard of what the shepherds saw;
In Birmingham we've got no sheep,
We get no peace and little sleep,
There's rubbish piled up in a heap,
There's loneliness to make you weep,
There's laughter, but the joy don't keep.

I've heard of Bethlehem before,
and Jesus, sleeping on the floor;
But Birmingham is more my town,
with feather bed and eiderdown,
pyjamas and a dressing-gown.
It's strange that Jesus' way was down,
yet painters show Him with a crown . . .

I've heard of Bethlehem before
but Birmingham suits me much more.
We get no angels singing there,
we get no shepherds in our hair,
no midday sun, no midnight glare

from stars that oughtn't to be there;
God doesn't know, God doesn't care.

I'VE HEARD OF BIRMINGHAM BEFORE,
I'VE OFTEN KNOCKED UPON YOUR DOOR;
MY SON HAS WALKED ALONG YOUR STREET,
WITH BLEEDING HANDS AND BLEEDING FEET.

*   *   *

Richard's problem isn't insoluble. He can have a new Dad.
If God can't solve Richard's problem then he won't be able
to do much with my problems, because my problems are
very much like Richard's. The biggest problems, the problems *we* can't solve, are *people*-problems. And God does set
out to deal with just these problems. The Good News does
set out to make men new, to make new men. Jesus saw the
people of Palestine, loaded down with problems, and they
didn't know where to take them. Who cared for the little
man? Sheep without a shepherd, ants lost in the ant-hill,
anonymous citizens of megalopolis. And he was sorry for
them. More than that: he offered to help them.

'Take my yoke,' said Jesus.

The yoke was a piece of wood, about four feet long, with
two hollows carved in it, to fit smoothly over the necks of
the two oxen who were to plough together. A well-made
yoke added little to the load to be carried, but made a great
deal of difference to the work that could be done. A badly
made yoke could leave the necks of the oxen rubbed raw at
the end of a hard day's ploughing. Says the Carpenter:

'Come to me and I will give you rest – all of you who
work so hard beneath a heavy yoke. Wear my yoke – for it
fits perfectly – and let me teach you; for I am gentle and
humble, and you shall find rest for your souls.' (Matthew
11.28–30)

That's an extraordinary thing for Jesus to say: 'I am
humble.'

If anyone else said it, it would provide a guarantee that he
was anything *but* humble. Yet Jesus *was* humble. Humble
enough to come amongst us, like us, sharing our pains and
problems.

Back in the Old Testament, the Jews were slaves in Egypt. The Egyptians were frightened that the Jews would eventually outstrip them numerically and technologically. So they oppressed them. The Jews cried to God. The years went by and still they prayed and still there seemed to be no answer. It was eighty years before the answer was clear. But when God started to give Moses his training in leadership, not in a university, but amongst the sheep, God said to Moses:

'I have seen the deep sorrows of my people in Egypt, and have heard their pleas for freedom from their harsh taskmasters. I have come to deliver them.' (Exodus 3.7–8)

That's the great thing: it is God who comes down to deliver us. God *knows!*

The article describing the following experiment gives a warning against drawing any human parallels from what happened, but I'll draw conclusions anyway. The experiment was carried through at the University of Georgia. Rats were trained to obtain food for themselves by pressing on a lever. They were offered two levers and both gave food. One was stiff to operate. The second was easy to operate. But when the easy-to-operate lever was pressed it not only gave food, it also gave the rats in the *next* cage a severe electric shock.

The experimenters had two lots of rats. The first group of rats had been in the second cage and experienced the electric shocks. The second group of rats had never felt an electric shock. When it came to getting their food, there was a clear difference between the behaviour of the two groups of rats. The rats that had never felt the electric shock pressed the easy-to-operate lever, apparently oblivious to the obvious distress of the rats in the next cage. The rats that had felt the electric shocks chose the hard-to-operate lever.

Pain, suffering, is one of the given experiences of life in this world. Volumes have been written about it, and yet we still don't pretend to understand it. We have just this way of light: God has experienced it too.

Maybe we can't write to him. The Post Office can't deliver Richard's letter. But if I can't write to him, he has written to me ... to Richard. We need someone to read the letter to Richard.

TALKING IT OVER

1. There has been an accident outside your church. A car has knocked a little girl down. She is very seriously hurt. What is the Good News for the father of the little girl? What is the Good News for the driver of the car? You are in church when the accident happens. What do you do?

2. Try to think yourself into the thirty or so years of life in Nazareth as a carpenter's son that Jesus had. What experiences of ours would he be able to identify with?

CHAPTER 11

Postscript for Parents

With all the mass of problems that face the world today, potentially the most disastrous is the dissolution of the family. Abortion, the pill, trial marriage, delinquency, all point back to the collapse of the family life. The family is the God-ordained foundation of every level of life:

the whole family of man, the *one* world

the family that is a nation

the village family . . . and a high-rise block can be a
  village

the church family

the husband-wife-children family.

Dr Tozer used to say: Some things are not negotiable. Well, the family is not negotiable. The marriage service says that marriage 'was ordained for the welfare of society, which can be strong and happy only when the marriage bond is held in honour'.

But the developing society carries within it pressures which tend to lead to the collapse of the family. The television set used to draw the family together in a sort of silent group worship. The car used to transport the family in a sealed-in package of steel and glass. And now that TV has lost its magnetism a pseudo-prosperity has handed the young folks the key to the car. And so the family dissolves, to meet, maybe, at meals.

This collapse of the family is not mandatory. We are not machines. We can turn off the TV. We can garage the car and use our legs. We can talk. Play together. Pray together. We are not machines. I was visiting a friend in the heyday of television. She was sitting, gloomily peering at the little box:

'I'm afraid there isn't much on tonight. It's really hopeless isn't it?' all in a hopeless kind of voice, still looking at the screen.

'It is. Why don't you turn it off?'

She looked at me, quite surprised. The thought had simply not occurred to her.

'Turn it off? . . . Yes, I suppose I could.'

And she did.

Then we were able to talk.

Jesus gave us a revolutionary picture of the family. He directs us to the eternal significance of the family as he addresses God, quite simply, as 'Father'. As he himself chooses to come amongst us as part of a working-class family, living in a rather nondescript village, Nazareth, and involved in a necessary but uninfluential job, carpentry. And, probably, shepherding. Most families in his day had their few sheep, and like David before him Jesus as a boy would have been sent out to watch them. When he was twelve years old he went with Mary and Joseph to Jerusalem, and when they returned to Nazareth he went with them. Luke records a remarkable comment on his relationship to them: 'He went down with them, and came to Nazareth, *and was obedient to them.*' (Luke 2.51 RSV)

It is John who records the same pattern of obedience *to God*: '. . . the Son can do nothing of his own accord, but only what he sees the Father doing.' (John 5.19 RSV)

It is this pattern of obedience, obedience of child to father, that is passed on to us in our family relationships.

But that isn't all. Jesus demonstrates the relationship between husband and wife by revealing the relationship which exists between himself and the church. I don't think that we should picture here the 'ideal' church, the 'abstract' church, the church as it ought to be, but the church as it really is. The relationship between Jesus and this church is simply that Jesus loves the church. Despite her blemishes. Despite, even, the occasional ugliness of the church. He still loves the church. And Paul dares to take up this fact and say: *that* is the relationship that ought to exist between husband and wife. The husband ought to love his wife, and that love has nothing really to do with time's inevitable process of uglification!

So we get two strands of teaching about the family: love and obedience. And we aren't allowed to say that this is merely a matter of culture. That obedience was all right for children in the eighteenth century but now we are liberated from such archaic notions. God, in Jesus, obeyed. Obeyed God, his Father, and obeyed Mary and Joseph. This is an eternal principle.

And it is not surprising if the Devil tries to undermine these two principles in his attacks on the family. Away with obedience! Love is a delusion!

LIFE WITH FATHER

The stage becomes a classroom for parents, to teach parents the principles underlying the destruction of the family. The teacher is trendy, loud. The students are brash self-assertive. The students are fooling around, talking, making a noise. The teacher comes in and the students take their places, still talking amongst themselves . . .

TEACHER: (*shouts*) Keep quiet can't you! I do my best to try to help you and all you seem able to do is behave as though you've never seen the inside of a classroom before . . . You . . . McGlashen, repeat that last phrase of mine adapted so as to make your children sore . . .

MCGLASHEN: (*snap response*) You children never seem to learn. I slave away all day to keep the house nice and all you can do is to behave like a bunch of hooligans who have never seen a decent home . . .

TEACHER: That's good, that's good. Next . . . Crossman . . . the three fundamentals of frustration.

CROSSMAN: (*gets to his feet, slowly; ticks off the three principles on his fingers*)
One, fudge the rules;
two, forget your promises;
three . . .

114

TEACHER: Come on, come on . . . Good night, you can't remember anything I tell you more than ten seconds. I must have told you a million times . . .

CROSSMAN: Okay, Okay, I've got it. Fantastic exaggeration.

TEACHER: You just made it. That's right, fudge the rules, forget your promises, fantastic exaggeration. Three ways to guarantee frustrated children.

Next . . . that's you, Doubleday. Come on up to the blackboard and outline the diamond analogy of family conflict.

DOUBLEDAY: (*goes to the blackboard, sketches the diagram, returns to his place.*)

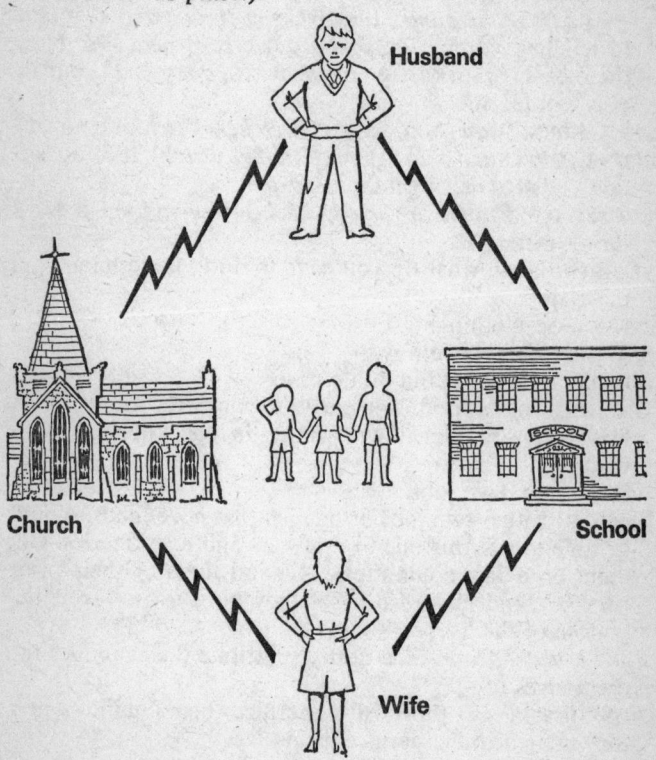

TEACHER: Right! Now do you all see the point? Parents criticise everybody at the church and the teachers at the school, but from opposite points of view so that they can also criticise each other. This teaches the children how to despise all authority so that eventually they deduce that they don't have to obey their parents. Or their teachers. In this way your children will learn patterns of conflict which will serve them well throughout their lives. *You* fight with *your* husbands and wives and *they* will fight with theirs. This way you can really influence generations that aren't even born yet.

Next, the psychology of terminological inexactitudes ... (*class looks blank; they whisper to one another*) How to tell lies, stupid. Only you don't *call* them lies. Now, three excuses for NOT doing what yesterday you promised you WOULD do:

MCGLASHEN: (*stands up, yawns, stretches*) I'm too tired ...

CROSSMAN: (*stands up, glances at his watch*) It's too late now ... we'd never get there in time ...

DOUBLEDAY: (*stands up; shakes his head solemnly*) Oh, but I didn't mean that.

TEACHER: Now, what do you have to do to undermine your marriage?

CROSSMAN: Nothing!

TEACHER: That's one way.

DOUBLEDAY: Cleave but don't leave.

TEACHER: That's good. You cleave to your wife but you don't leave your mother. Two women in one kitchen! It's a certainty!

MCGLASHEN: Two jobs.

TEACHER: Either two jobs or one job that never ends. You'll be able to sell this one to ministers and missionaries. Get them on a few committees. Remind them of their priorities ... and make sure that they put *themselves* at the bottom of the list ...

DOUBLEDAY: ... and then neatly substitute their families for themselves ...

CROSSMAN: ... so they really sacrifice their families when they imagine they sacrifice themselves.

116

MCGLASHEN: Little habits.

TEACHER: Such as?

CROSSMAN: Leaving the top off the toothpaste . . .

MCGLASHEN: . . . humming at dinner time . . .

DOUBLEDAY: . . . a tie that doesn't match . . .

CROSSMAN: . . . a sniff . . .

DOUBLEDAY: Leaving the doors open . . .

TEACHER: . . . taken with our Fantastic Exaggeration: 'You *always* leave the top off the toothpaste', 'You *always* leave *all* the doors open', 'You *always* sniff like that', when in fact no one is ever consistent enough to do anything *always*.

Well . . . work on it. Or, if that doesn't work, *don't* work on it, and any marriage can be made to fail.

Now let's repeat our College song together: (*recite or sing*)

We'll alter our rules though we made them this morning

We'll break every promise as soon as it's made,

We'll change our intentions without any warning,

We'll undermine marriage and not be afraid

to use every twisted and tortuous plan

to ruin the home and to undermine man.

WHAT THE BIBLE SAYS

Psalm 68.6
He gives families to the lonely.

Ephesians 3.14–16
When I think of the wisdom and scope of his plan I fall down on my knees and pray to the Father of all the great family of God – some of them already in heaven and some down here on earth – that out of his glorious, unlimited resources he will give you the mighty inner strengthening of his Holy Spirit.

Ephesians 5.21–6.4 (RSV)

BE SUBJECT TO ONE ANOTHER OUT OF REVERENCE FOR CHRIST.
Wives, be subject to your husbands, as to the Lord. For the
husband is the head of the wife as Christ is the head of the
church, his body, and is himself its Saviour. As the church
is subject to Christ, so let wives also be subject in everything
to their husbands. Husbands, love your wives, as Christ
loved the church and gave himself up for her, that he might
sanctify her, having cleansed her by the washing of water
with the word, that he might present the church to himself in
splendour, without spot or wrinkle or any such thing, that
she might be holy and without blemish. Even so husbands
should love their wives as their own bodies. He who loves
his wife loves himself. For no man ever hates his own flesh,
but nourishes it and cherishes it, as Christ does the church,
because we are members of his body. 'For this reason a man
shall leave his father and mother and be joined to his wife,
and the two shall become one.' This mystery is a profound
one, and I am saying that it refers to Christ and the church;
however, let each one of you love his wife as himself, and let
the wife see that she respects her husband.

Children, obey your parents in the Lord, for this is right.

'Honour your father and mother' (this is the first commandment with a promise), 'that it may be well with you
and that you may live long on the earth'. Fathers, do not
provoke your children to anger, but bring them up in the
discipline and instruction of the Lord.

LEAVING AND CLEAVING

Marriage is sometimes described as a *creation ordinance*.
Marriage was part of the creation story. Right at the start
the principle of marriage is established. Notice what is said
about it:

   'It isn't good for man to be alone.' (Genesis 2.18)
   'A man leaves his father and mother.' (Genesis 2.24)
   'A man is joined to his wife in such a way that the two
   become one person.' (Genesis 2.24)

118

These are three vitally important principles. It isn't good to be alone. Marriage is the answer. But a man grows up with responsibility towards his parents. He leaves them, that is the answer. He marries a wife. The two cannot be lonely, for they are one person and that is the answer.

We'll look at these three principles, one at a time.

Why is it not good for a person to be alone? The question isn't clearly answered anywhere in the Bible, but the curious and mysterious doctrine of the Trinity has a bearing on the answer. It is rather as if God is saying to us: 'It is not good that even I should be alone.'

We don't have to think of the Trinity as three elderly gentlemen perched precariously on a cloud as a kind of heavenly debating society. But the Christian doctrine of the Trinity most certainly presents us with a warmer picture of God than the stern picture of the only, lonely Allah of Islam. And again, we can't think of the three Persons of the Trinity without thinking of them as in conversation. Jesus *asks* the Father who then *tells* the Spirit to come to the church. Jesus acts as our defending counsel when we are accused to the Father (1 John 2.1). The Spirit intercedes for us when we pray, interpreting our spiritual thinking to the Father (Romans 8.26).

This ought to provide us with the answer to the question of why it is not good for us to be alone. Like God we need to talk!

But talking is dangerous. We very often misunderstand one another. That is the whole art of politics: either to talk but say nothing, or to talk and be completely lucid, absolutely clear. I'm reminded of the two Members of Parliament who went for a drive in the country and got lost. They stopped in a very small village and asked one of the villagers:

'Excuse me, but where *are* we?'

The man looked them up and down and then replied, tongue in cheek: 'Well, you're in your car right now!'

And the driver turned to his friend and commented: 'Now that was the perfect parliamentary reply. It was short, it was true and it didn't tell us anything we didn't know already!'

It's when you really want to say something important that the imperfections of human communication become apparent. We simply don't understand one another. We mis-hear words, misunderstand motives, misinterpret intonation and end up in disarray.

Now God doesn't do that. The Trinity has it both ways: three Persons so that they may commune, talk, converse, but only one God so that the three share fully in all the input. And God has arranged the same for man. Marriage. Two people becoming one, and yet retaining the privilege of conversation, discussion, even distinctness. One yet two. Just as God is three yet One.

Husband and wife share their lives in a way that is impossible to all others. They are freed from the undesirable condition of loneliness.

But now the second point: *leaving*. Husband and wife are expected to leave their parents when they marry. A new unit comes into existence just as the new husband and the new wife were theatening the unity, the one-ness, of their parents. Children *do* tend to come between parents. And if that tendency exists at all it becomes more pronounced as the children get older. The mother dotes on the son more and more, leaving her husband more and more alone. The father spoils his daughter more and more, leaving his wife dowdy and neglected.

Actually we seem to put a great deal of strain on the whole of our family life by expecting children to delay marriage until they can furnish the house and provide a forty-eight inch TV and put a car into the garage, or until they can complete the BA-MA-PH.D ladder. The youngsters find it difficult to hold on to our moral standards that long, and modern trends encourage them to abandon morality anyway, and at the same time the pressure on the parents keeps mounting up. It's not really surprising that the parents' marriages tend to break up when at long last the children *do* leave. The 'empty-nest syndrome' has the parents suddenly aware of the fact that when the children left the whole purpose of being alive walked out of the front door with them. And then the children's marriages tend to be short-lived, too, because they've been taught not that marriage is a marvellous thing, but that it's a nuisance: 'tying you down, when you ought to be having fun' is the usual phrase. But marriage *is* fun, entered into when you are young enough not to be weighed down by responsibilities and healthy enough to be able to enjoy one another and travel around a bit.

But. Too many marriages don't leave. Mother comes too. Less frequently father. Now we have to be careful here. The Jews are a Semitic people and they had and still have what is called the extended family. Not just husband and wife and children, but with uncles and aunts and widowed mothers and the rest, all part of the 'family'. Not that they all lived together, but they were all part of the family. Leaving wasn't intended to mean abandoning. But the relationships all change. If mother comes too she does not come as mother-to-be-obeyed, but as mother-to-be-cared-for. Her son, who used to obey, is now head of the house. Her daughter, who used to get out of the kitchen when she was told to, now has the right to have the kitchen to herself. So the leaving is a special kind of leaving, and in particular it is not an abandoning, unless it is an abandoning of a now defunct relationship.

Thirdly *cleaving*. Husband and wife are joined together. Now, of course, that does mean the sexual relationship. But that is not the whole of it. This particular verse is considered so important that it appears in the Bible five times:

Genesis 2.24
Matthew 19.5 and Mark 10.7–8
1 Corinthians 6.16
Ephesians 5.31

The first reference establishes the basic principles of marriage. Matthew–Mark and 1 Corinthians all deal with the possibility of a marriage breaking up, through divorce or through immorality. The point is being made clear: two become one and this is a permanent union. Cleave together.

But marriage brings with it certain stresses. Disagreements come. Age brings change. The slim husband develops

121

a paunch. The Bible says: cleave together. Not because you are 'in love' but just because. This is C. S. Lewis again:

> In the humans the Enemy (God) has gratuitously as-sociated affection between the (married) parties with sexual desire. He has also made the offspring dependent on the parents and given the parents an impulse to sup-port it – thus producing the family, which is like the organism only worse; for the members are more distinct, yet also united in a more conscious and responsible way. The whole thing, in fact, turns out to be simply one more device for dragging in Love.
>
> Now comes the joke. The Enemy described a married couple as 'one flesh'. He didn't say 'a happily married couple' or 'a couple who married because they were in love', but you can make the humans ignore that. You can also make them forget that the man they call Paul did not confine it to *married* couples. Mere copulation, for him, makes 'one flesh'.
>
> You can thus get the humans to accept as rhetorical eulogies of 'being in love' what were, in fact, plain de-scriptions of the real significance of sexual intercourse. The truth is that wherever a man lies with a woman, there, whether they like it or not, a transcendental relationship is set up between them which must be eternally enjoyed or eternally endured.
>
> From the true statement that this transcendental rela-tionship was intended to produce (and, if entered into obediently, too often *will* produce) affection and the family, humans can be made to infer the false belief that the blend of affection, fear and desire which they call 'being in love' is the only thing that makes marriage either happy or holy.
>
> (*Screwtape Letters*)

Do you see? In the West we expect people to 'fall in love' and then get married. In the east the couple get married and then fall in love.

As a consequence *we* sometimes reason: 'The world doesn't go *clunk!* when he kisses me now, so we obviously don't love one another and how can you justify marriage without love?'

The biblical answer to which is that cleaving is the justification for marriage. Bible-type loving is a *product* of marriage, not the *cause* of marriage.

So love, Bible-style, may appear before marriage or it may develop after marriage but its non-appearance indicates merely a failure of husband or wife to work at the marriage. It doesn't indicate the collapse of the marriage.

There's the point. Marriage is to be worked at. It needs attention. Precisely because it is so fundamental to God's eternal plan for us it is also a prime target of Satan. Tragically it is often precisely the most devoted workers for God whose marriages succumb to Satanic attack. Ministers whose marriages are a sad charade. Missionaries who accept long periods of separation from their families, ostensibly 'for the work's sake', but often simply because the marriage no longer has any attraction for them. Love doesn't produce the perfect marriage. The perfect marriage produces love! And the perfect marriage is one where husband and wife *know* that they don't want to be alone: they want to be together. Where they have learned to *leave* the old relationships and where they are determined, through thick and thin, to *cleave* to one another.

But what about the single person? Well, it is still not good for you to be alone. It does take courage to move out and form relationships, but it is essential to do so. Of course there's the church. That *ought* to be a family, but with our determination to count success by the size of the congregation, very few churches are families. And if they are family size someone is sure to get to work to make them grow!

But a biblical-love relationship is still possible for the single person. Without homosexuality. *That* is unbiblical. But David had such a fine relationship to Jonathan, that his comment when Jonathan died was simple:

Jonathan is slain upon the hills.
How I weep for you, my brother Jonathan;
How much I loved you!
Your love for me was deeper
Than the love of women.

David was an oft-married man. But in fact he found the greatest Bible-love in his friendship with Jonathan. There need be no element of homosexuality in such a relationship at all. Deep friendships *can* be forged by the single person. But again: such friendships are easily broken, and need to be worked at; Satan would have us lost, isolated pin-points in the mass of humanity. God still seeks to set us in families. It is *not* good to be alone.

We may not enjoy living permanently in a crowd. We all need to be aware of the danger of being alone.

TALK IT OVER

1. Write down a dozen or so habits, customs, experiences, practices that you have seen producing tensions and problems in people's marriages.

   How could these problems be tackled?

   What happens if they're not tackled?
2. What are the advantages and disadvantages of 'falling in love' *before* getting married?
3. Think about one marriage that seems to you about ideal. What makes it tick?
4. What special pressures are there on the marriages of ministers and missionaries?

   What does your church do to protect such people from these pressures? What could be done?
5. You fall into one or other of the following categories:
   just about to be married/expecting to be married
   married already
   parents with children soon to be married
   single

Since the Bible says flatly that it's *not* good to be alone, what do you do to ensure obedience to the Bible on this point? How do you relate to your own marriage or other people's marriages?

Recent Lakeland paperbacks

BATTLE FOR AFRICA
Brother Andrew

A world-wide war is being fought this very minute. Even though you may not be aware of it, you are irretrievably involved. If you choose not to engage the enemy where he is now he will attack you here at home. Military weapons are useless against this enemy. His attack strikes at a deeper level than the arenas of politics, economics and the military. His battlefield is a spiritual one, and his goal is to change and control men's minds.

But the Church stands in the way of this enemy. The front line of this battle is Africa. Brother Andrew explains how Christians in the free world can play their part in overcoming the enemy.

LOVE HAS COME AGAIN
Jim Bigelow

Man was not made to be alone. We were made to live in loving relationship with both God and one another. However, the hero of the Western world is portrayed as the self-sufficient loner. By equating independence with maturity, man's basic nature is denied. Can the Church bring healing to those torn between what they are and what they feel they should be? Jim Bigelow believes the Church has the answer which he outlines clearly in this book, with many personal examples.

THINK AGAIN
Frank Thewlis

Frank Thewlis's broadcasts in 'Pause for Thought' on BBC Radio 2 have been heard by millions. Now the most popular of these talks, showing that God is not only to be found in churches but in the most ordinary situations of our common life, are available in book form.

Recent Lakeland paperbacks

CRY OF THE HUMAN HEART
Juan Carlos Ortiz

Most Christians think they are living in the New Covenant. But they are not. Instead, they have made of the New Testament a set of rules and they are trying to fulfil these laws in the flesh. This misconception, Juan Carlos Ortiz believes, accounts for much of the spiritual defeat which Christians experience. They are frustrated, disappointed with themselves because they cannot fulfil that deepest cry of their hearts – to please God.

What is the way out of this dilemma? That is what the book is all about.

LIFE IN THE OVERLAP
Jean Darnall

Designed to help the reader understand the purpose of personal spiritual struggle. In presenting spiritual patterns of successful living for the Christian caught in the overlap between Human Experience and Biblical Revelation, the author enables the reader to develop the desire to go on and resolve these inner conflicts.

ELDRIDGE CLEAVER: ICE AND FIRE!
George Otis

Former Black Power militant, Eldridge Cleaver, faces trial on charges arising from violent Black Panther confrontation with the police in 1968. Until last year Cleaver dodged trial by going into political exile. Finally, having visited the Meccas of his communist ideology, he settled in France, but it was not optimism that filled his soul but despair. In looking out at the vastness of the universe he came to believe in something more – God.

Recent Lakeland paperbacks

FOR THIS CROSS I'LL KILL YOU
Bruce Olson

'Don't go near them,' said the woman on the bus. 'They'll kill you.' But I was confident – and excited at beginning a new adventure.

Nineteen-year-old Bruce Olson knew God had called him to live with the Motilone Indians in the Colombian jungle. How did he survive the years of sickness, rejection and desperate loneliness which followed, until at least he won the confidence of the Motilone people, and learned how to bring them the message of Christ without destroying their culture?

It was for the cross that he loved the Motilones and became loved in return. But was it also for the cross that he or his first convert would die?

BREAKOUT
Fred Lemon with Gladys Knowlton

It was very quiet in my cell after the warder had escorted me back from the 'dungeons' – the punishment cells. I threw myself on the hard bed, a black bitterness of soul filling me. Tomorrow, I vowed, I would get hold of the sharpest knife in the mailbag room – and there would be murder done. Weary and tormented I pulled the coarse blanket round my shoulders and closed my eyes.

Something made me sit up suddenly. There were three men in the cell with me; they were dressed in ordinary civvy suits. The man on the right spoke:

'Fred,' he said, 'This is Jesus . . .'

Fred Lemon, a confirmed criminal, on the eve of attempting to break out of Dartmoor, unexpectedly broke out spiritually, and found this freedom far greater than that of the open moor.

This story of an East End child who grows into a violent criminal, simply and powerfully shows how criminality breeds and takes a man step by step into the abandonment of hell, and yet how Christ can meet a man even there.